KENDALL McDONALD made the first of his many wreck dives in Kent waters in April 1961. The wreck was that of the great five-masted sailing ship *Preussen*, lost in Crab Bay, near Dover, in November 1910. The author of more than 30 books, mostly about wrecks and diving, Kendall McDonald is a former chairman of the British Sub-Aqua Club and now a Vice President. A veteran diving journalist, he is a regular contributor to DIVER magazine and is that journal's editorial consultant on wrecks and wreck diving.

© Copyright 1994
by Underwater World Publications Ltd
55 High Street, Teddington, Middlesex TW11 8HA

Cover photograph of excavation work on the 1809 wreck *Admiral Gardner* (see site 262) by Richard Larn.

Maps by Suzanne Hall

Location photography by Roy Smallpage

Other illustrations courtesy of: Tim Bennetto (pp. 27, 73); BT Pictures (p. 48); Illustrated London News (pp. 42, 57); Imperial War Museum (pp. 53, 54); Richard Larn (p. 99); National Maritime Museum (pp. 23, 29, 43, 61, 80, 103, 105, 131).

Book produced by DIVER Magazine
and printed by Emirates Printing Press,
PO Box 5106, Airport Road, Dubai, UAE.

ISBN: 0 946020 20 5

In the same series:

Contents

Preface

The divers of Kent and experts on every aspect of Kent seagoing life have generously given their time and their knowledge to this book and everyone who dives or plans to dive Kent will thank them for that.

Some contributors ranged so widely in their Kent diving that it is impossible to attribute their information to one particular area in these acknowledgements. Some have specialised in one particular wreck or patch of sea. Every detail has been vital to the production of this book and so I have thanked them here by name and in some cases areas, but this does not mean that their information has been confined to that particular area.

❏ Dave Batchelor, Bob Jessop, Colin Cole, Peter Weatherly, the late Brud Martin and the divers of Folkestone BSAC.

❏ Vic Hooker, Clive Surridge, John Abbatt , Mick Lucas and the divers of Canterbury BSAC.

❏ Bob Peacock and the divers of Thanet BSAC.

❏ Dave Chamberlain, of Walmer, skipper of dive boat *Morning Haze*.

❏ Dave Harris, of Walmer, skipper of dive boat *Moss Rose*.

❏ John Chamberlain of the East Kent Maritime Trust of Ramsgate and his wife Diane of Ramsgate Maritime Museum.

❏ Lieutenant Commander J.D. Pugh RN and Mrs. Francine Ashford of the Wreck Section of the Hydrographic Department of the Ministry of Defence.

❏ Richard Larn, for Goodwins diving expertise and the *Admiral Gardner*.

❏ Staff Officer Eric Musson, of HM Coastguard Channel Navigation Information Service.

❏ Peter Brown, HM Coastguard Sport Diving Liaison Officer.

❏ Kingsdown BSAC divers

❏ Dover BSAC divers.

❏ Captain Peter White, Harbourmaster, Dover.

❏ David Church and the staff of the Dover Harbour Board.

❏ Paul James, Chairman of the Folkestone Fishermen's Association.

❏ Miss S. Murphy of the Kent and Essex Sea Fisheries Committee.

❏ Christopher Davies of the Department of the Environment.

❏ Martin Dean of the Archaeological Diving Unit.

❑ Dr.Mark Redknap for details of work on the *Stirling Castle, Northumberland* and *Restoration* on the Goodwins.
❑ Tim Bennetto of the dive boat *Cirrus*.
❑ David Green and the divers of Maidstone BSAC.
❑ Tony Goodfellow of Gillingham for the *Toward* and other mined ships.
❑ Paul Fletcher, diver-skipper of the *Stella Spei* of Ramsgate.
   Though those named have made important contributions to this book, there are scores of others who gave small but vital information whom I have no room here to thank personally. The waters off the Kent coast provide exciting and rewarding diving. I hope this book will help all divers to enjoy them even more.

KENDALL McDONALD

How to use this book

In this book the coastline of Kent – from Margate to the Sussex border to the west of Dungeness – has been divided into six areas from west to east (see map overleaf). Each area has a separate chapter containing a guide to diving, spot by spot, wreck by wreck, but also the back-up information vital to divers. This includes launch sites, harbour information and useage, radio channels, Admiralty chart numbers, Ordnance Survey maps, and important local details.

The BSAC branches to contact for local help are collected together in an appendix at the end of the book. Other appendices give details of air supplies, dive boats, and sources for weather information and the Military Remains Act of 1986.

All depths are given in metres. All distances are in miles. All dimensions of ships are in feet. Tonnages are gross. Admiralty charts are the metric versions. Ordnance Survey maps are 1:50,000 or about 1¼in to the mile. Positions given are *not,* repeat *not,* metric.

The contents page lists the six areas into which Kent has been split for easy reference. Each of the six area chapters follows the same format. First, a short introduction describes the area and notes any points of importance. Here you will find the local launching sites. Any shore dives (of which there are very few in Kent) are listed among the boat diving sites which are described in detail. The number of each site is shown on the area map at the start of each chapter.

Practically all Kent diving is boat diving. In this book no distinction has been made between modern inflatable diving and hard-boat diving. This should *not* be taken to mean that all sites can be prudently reached by inflatable – in the same way, the few shore dive sites are intended only for the strong swimmer on the calmest of calm days.

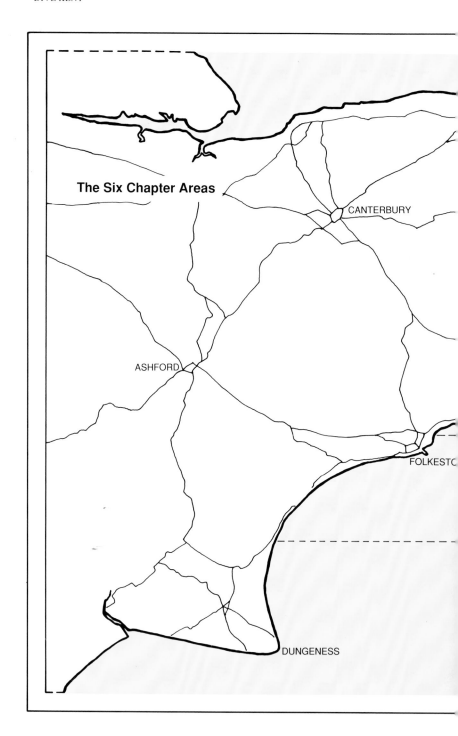

The Six Chapter Areas

CANTERBURY

ASHFORD

FOLKESTC

DUNGENESS

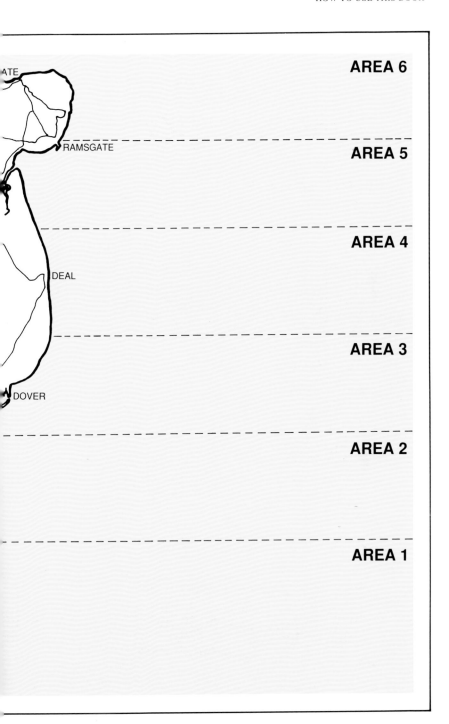

ATE

RAMSGATE

AREA 6

AREA 5

AREA 4

DEAL

AREA 3

DOVER

AREA 2

AREA 1

Inner and Outer Harbours, Folkestone.

The dive planner's guide to Kent

The wrecks

The Kent coastline is a wreck diver's paradise. There are more wrecks in these waters than any other part of Britain. The Channel has always been the last ditch of our defences and as a result the Straits of Dover have been a regular battleground for ships of many nations. The casualties of these engagements litter the seabed, put there by mines, torpedoes from U-boats, E-boats and destroyers, cannonballs, grapeshot and mortar shells, fireships, shellfire, machine gun fire, rockets and cannonshells from aircraft, bombs from dive bombers, airships and boarding parties. Not all of these munitions exploded so divers exploring any ship should take great care.

However, not everything on the seabed is there as a result of malice. The Kent coastline has fierce tides and sometimes violent storms. In the days of sail, anchorages such as the Downs were supposed to give shelter to ships of all kinds which used the Channel as a main trade route, but many of them perished just when they thought they were safe. Some were torn out of the anchorages and blown right over to the Goodwins. Not that the Goodwins had to rely on storms. The "great ship swallower" gobbled many a ship whose captain made a navigational error on a calm day. At a conservative estimate, over 2500 ships have been lost "on the Goodwins" since records began.

Although the Goodwins have such a shocking reputation, there are thousands more ships sunk in the coastal waters off the Kent coast which were lost without ever seeing the Goodwins rise up out of the sea at them. Many of these losses were due to the huge quantity of shipping being forced into the squeeze of the Dover Straits and the number of collisions which resulted – and still do occur, even in today's world of strict shipping lanes and radar on both ship and shore. The Dover Straits are the busiest shipping waters in the world,which makes diving in these narrows a matter of careful planning and skillful operation.

The weather

The weather which affects diving off the east coast of Kent is, to say the least,

variable. As any local resident will tell you, and the Met Office will confirm, it all depends on the winds. So when in Kent you should know that:
– south-west winds bring cloudy and damp weather, with rain and gales during the winter;
– north-west winds bring showers and bright periods, with occasional squalls;
– winds from the east and south bring warm and dry weather in summer, but really cold winters.

The Kent coast from North Foreland to Dungeness can suffer some very violent weather. Huge seas pile up to the west of the narrow Dover Straits during gales from south-west and west. In the Straits themselves the effect on the sea of strong winds from north-east and south-west funnelling through the narrows is dramatic. Then great swells force even the cross-Channel ferries to stop. This sort of weather has guaranteed that over the centuries the Straits have become known as "Shipwreck Alley".

The north-east winds, most frequent from January to April, are particularly deadly, raising massive breakers on the sandbanks to the north of Dover. Fortunately for divers this type of rough sea doesn't often occur between April and October. The really rough weather comes to the area when depressions move north and north-east from September to March and weather from Northern Europe can bring below zero temperatures as late as March.

Sudden sea fogs can come with warm south-west and west winds. These almost-total whiteouts are worst in the Straits and are slow to clear. On average, the diver cox'n should be prepared for three such fogs in each of the months of April, May and June, two in July, one in August and one in September. February is the worst of the winter months, with an average of seven.

Very warm weather between March and August is usually followed by a period of lower temperatures as depressions come to Britain from the Atlantic. No British diver will be surprised to learn that sea temperatures off Kent are coldest in February and warmest in August.

The winds rule diving in Kent.The main points to remember are: most winds come from the south-west and north-west; north to north-east winds are most frequent from February to May; south-west and north-east winds are boosted by being squeezed through the Straits and bring rough seas on either side; there is little shelter from winds from the south-east and south-west along the coast from Dungeness to Folkestone.

Gales, which can reach 80 knots, are likely in this area if other areas are being treated more gently with winds of 5-6 from the south-west or north-east. Gales on average occur on Kent's east coast as follows: January – four; February – three; March – three; April – two; May – one, June to August none; September – one, October – two; November – three; December – four.

Believe it or not, there is less rain, and shorter periods of it, on the Kent coast of the Channel than there is on the coastline of counties further to the west. Even so, thunderstorms with sudden squalls and the odd waterspout average two a month from May to September.

However, one basic rule is no different in Kent than anywhere else: the average wind speed is greater at sea than on land. Anyone planning a dive in the area should take advantage of the Met Office marine forecasting services. Details of both Marinecall and MetFAX services are given in the appendices at the back of this book.

Visibility

There are those who speak with horror of Kent diving, talking of black water and telling "couldn't even see my fingertips pressed against my mask" stories. If you meet any of these characters you can safely assume that they have never dived Kent, or if they have, they picked a bad day. Of course, Kent has its poor vis days just like anywhere else and strong tides and soft bottoms can produce more of them here than in more favoured spots further west. But Kent has its fantastic vis days too, and I was struck when talking to local divers how often they described being able to see almost the whole length of a ship! Generally, the closer inshore you are the less is the vis. The good vis is usually about 2 miles out and further. It is also fair to say that the waters south of Folkestone are more likely to be silty than those further north. Early May often produces "Maywater" with the vis ruined by plankton, but the rest of May and June usually produce excellent visibility. This clear vis may again be cut down by plankton in August only to return again in the autumn.

However, there are some certainties. You can take it as read that if an east wind blows, the vis goes too. It is also true that if a north-east wind blows hard, the vis disappears, but a south-westerly puts the vis back. Visibility on the Goodwins is dealt with in Area 4.

Depths

Apart from the deeps east of The Varne and to the east of the Goodwins, there is little in excess of 40m in the Dover Strait area; and generally in the areas covered by this book, depths do not exceed 50m. Sandwaves do alter depths in the Northern or other named areas.

Springs of up to 4 knots occur in the Dover Straits, but elsewhere 2 to 2.5 knots is rarely exceeded. Neaps at Dover are about 3.3m; springs at Dover are about 5.9m. At Margate, neaps average 2.5m; springs average 4.3m.

Divers and fishermen

Kent divers and local fishermen enjoy very good relations with each other, and every diver in these waters should do his or her best to keep it that way. Local divers answer every request for help to recover fouled gear and as a result have been guided to many formerly "unknown" wrecks. In fact all the historic wreck finds in the area have come about as a result of this good relationship – a fisherman would come to the divers with a tale of old wood in his nets or a fouled trawl or net which needed untangling and lo and behold, they found an ancient wreck! Of course, those who have helped to release fouled gear for the fishermen know, as do the fishermen themselves, that this is no easy task, often deep and dark and no place for the novice.

The whole coast is heavily fished, with most potting concentrated inside the 20m line along Hythe Bay and East Wear Bay to Shakespeare Cliff, Dover. Main catches are crab, lobster and whelks, a local delicacy. Divers should be aware that netting has increased greatly in recent years and is carried out from close inshore out to about 3 miles, in places where the beam trawlers do not operate. There is a steady trawling effort though, in the same waters. Dover sole (of course!), lemon sole and plaice are well fished and supply the local hotel trade as well as many retail outlets. But the skate, turbot and brill fishery has dwindled. Paul James, chairman of the Folkestone Fishermen's Association, says that it is now a "minnow" of its former self. Cod, whiting, pollack and dogfish are the other main species. Catches in general have declined.

In the Northern section of the area, things are slightly different. Here whelking is the major potting industry with crabs and lobsters caught more in nets. Gill netting is widespread with the major catches being of plaice and sole and a good deal of netting inshore. Catching turbot and brill are bonuses rather than the norm. There is a good trawling effort. Skate fishing is holding up well. The skate and bass are caught on the Goodwins and Margate Sands. Tommy Brown, secretary of the Thanet Fishermen's Association, stresses their good relations with divers and asked that I should specially remind divers of the dangers of "phantom fishing nets" lost or abandoned on wrecks in the area.

The Kent and Essex Sea Fisheries Committee lays down minumum sizes for fish and shellfish in the area. At the time of going to press, these were the sizes, but obviously divers should check for any alterations:

FISH	(Measured from tip of snout to end of tail fin) cm	
Bass		36
Black bream		23
Blue ling		70
Brill		30
Cod		35
Conger Eel		58
Dab		23
Flounder		25
Grey mullet		30
Haddock		30
Hake		30
Herring		20
Lemon sole		25
Mackerel		30
Megrim		25
Plaice		27
Pollack		30
Red mullet		15
Red seabream		25
Saithe		35
Shad		30
Sole		24
Turbot		30
Whiting		27
Witch		28
Skates and rays	From wing tip to wing tip	35
Crab	Across the broadest part of back	12.5
Spider crab	Across the broadest part of back	12
Lobster	Rear of eye socket to rear end of body shell,	8.5
	or overall length	24

Note: A Kent and Essex Sea Fisheries bye-law forbids the taking of any berried lobster.

Using the Coastguard

The Coastguard stress what anyone intending to dive the area should know – diving in the Dover Straits is not for the inexperienced. To say that the Dover Straits are extremely busy at all times is a massive understatement. Each day as many as 500 ship movements of vessels crossing the Channel or in transit through the area are recorded. In an average 24-hour period, this means that there are 200 or more crossings by ferries and 150 ships going each way in the traffic lanes. These figures do not include fishing vessels, yachts and other pleasure boats.

The ship movements *do* include hydrofoils, catamarans, hovercraft and power-boats operating at speeds up to 60 knots. That doesn't include the tankers – up to half a mile long! - drawing 75ft; and travelling at up to 26 knots, which can create a wash 3ft high for 3 miles away from their course. Big ships will not, and usually cannot, divert for any dive boat anchored in their path. In fact it is laid down that vessels of less than 20m shall not impede vessels in the traffic lanes. To try to do so was compared by a coastguard senior watch officer at Dover as "like collecting mushrooms on the M25"!

The Coastguards want divers to use them, to involve them in the dive planning by telling them about your diving. They will want to know the following: WHERE do you intend to dive? WHEN do you intend to make that dive? HOW MANY divers are involved? Plus the telephone number of a contact onshore. Remember that they need to hear from you when your diving is completed. Such information can be passed to them by telephone, but the sensible diver will make sure that the dive boat carries VHF radio, so that you can talk to the Coastguard on Channels 16 (first), 67 and 80.

Dover Coastguard want to help, and their advice is available 24 hours a day. Diving Officers and Dive Marshals should contact Dover Coastguards in the early stages of the dive plan. Tel: 0304 210008.

All dive boats should of course carry all the recommended safety equipment, and all divers intending to dive the Dover Straits should regard a radar reflector on their dive boat as essential. No diving should take place without the A-flag being flown, but only when the actual diving is in progress.

The traffic lanes

On Monday January 11,1971, at 2am, a huge explosion rocked the Kent coast from Dungeness to North Foreland. No-one knew what had caused it until a fishing trawler off Folkestone reported seeing something like a fireball near the Varne Bank. The mystery was solved within minutes when the Liberian ship *Paracas* reported that she had been in collision with a tanker.

The first lifeboat to reach the spot found that the tanker, the *Texaco Caribbean,* had been blown in half by the explosion of part of her cargo. Fifteen of those aboard were dead and the rest of the *Texaco Caribbean's* oil was soon causing massive pollution all along the Kent coast.

A Trinity House ship was soon on the spot marking the wreck and shipping was warned by radio. Despite this, the next day the German cargo ship *Brandenburg* hit the wreck of the tanker and sank swiftly with the loss of 14 of her crew. Trinity House now put out no fewer than five wreck marker buoys and stationed a wreck marking vessel on the spot. But even this didn't stop the Greek ship *Niki* ploughing into the two wrecks. She sank too and all 22 of her crew were lost.

Fifty-one men had lost their lives in three days. The British Government acted quickly and in 1972 the Channel Navigation Information Service was started by HM Coastguard at St. Margaret's Bay, near Dover. Radar was installed and the first traffic separation scheme in the world was introduced. The figures for collisions in the Straits quickly declined. In 1973 an Anglo-French agreement was reached on swapping information about vessels using the Channel. The routing system jointly introduced by Britain and France meant that ships going to the North Sea and so to north-west Europe would keep to the French side and ships heading west down Channel would keep to the English side.

Rule 10 of the Collision Regulations governs the behaviour of ships in the Straits and is strictly enforced by both Britain and France. Vessels which do not obey the regulations are called "rogues" and are either identified by passing ships or the Coastguard spotter plane based at Manston, Kent. A computer plot of the offender's course through the Straits is kept, and this together with a video recording and a tape of any voice exchanges is sent to the Department of Transport so that the "rogue" can be prosecuted.

Divers and the traffic lanes

Divers will find the traffic lanes outlined in purple on their charts with little arrows indicating the direction of the traffic. Large purple patches mark the separation zones, but this does not mean that large vessels will not be encountered in them even though those collision regulations do require vessels "so far as is practicable" to keep clear of the traffic separation lines or separation zones.

Rule 10(j) of the Collision Regulations basically inhibits divers from diving in the traffic lanes. The rule states: "Sailing vessels and vessels under 20m in length shall not impede the safe passage of a power-driven vessel following a traffic lane", which the Coastguard interpret to mean that diving tenders should not stop in the north-east or south-west lanes, nor should divers operate in them. Matters are slightly different in separation zones such as the Varne Bank, but then divers should be aware that big ships will be found here at the top of the tide on occasions. If the dive boat must cross a traffic lane, the regulations of both the British and French say it should be done at right angles to the traffic flow.

As a result, most diving takes place in the Inshore Traffic Zone, which is not normally used by through traffic, and is designated for use by vessels under 20m in length and sailing ships of all kinds. But this, of course, does not mean that dive boats in this extremely busy area can relax. A strict lookout must be kept, recall signals must be carried at all times, a listening watch should be kept on VHF, and divers should listen to the CNIS broadcasts on Channel 11. The Channel Navigation Information Service (CNIS) is operated by the Coastguard and gives traffic and navigational reports of immediate interest as well as details of any "rogues" about. **Dover** broadcasts on Channel 11 VHF at 40 minutes past the hour. **Cap Gris Nez** broadcasts on Channel 11 VHF at 10 minutes past the hour.

These broadcasts usually last less than 10 minutes and do not normally include details of ferries crossing the Channel on regular routes. Nor do they usually include details of amateur diving operations, though commercial diving will be reported.

The Channel Navigation Information Service maintains a 24-hour listening watch on Channel 80 (call sign: "Dover Coastguard").

Sport diving will obviously take place not very far from Channel ferry routes. The noise of ferries when underwater – even when a long, long distance away – can be quite amazing. Local divers say that the Sea Cat is the noisiest of all.

Divers and the law

Most of Kent diving is wreck diving and many of the wrecks have military connections. This is where the diver should remember that the Military Remains Act became law on September 8,1986. The basic purpose of the Act was to preserve the sanctity of "war graves", that is the wreckage of military ships and aircraft known to contain human remains of Service personnel. No diver would disagree with that. For more details of how this affects divers in Kent seas, see Appendix 5.

AREA 1:

Dungeness to Littlestone

Admiralty chart No.1892   **Ordnance Survey map 189**

This area starts at the Sussex border at 00 51 24E and continues round the point of Dungeness to the Eastward where 51 00 00N crosses the coastline north of Littlestone-on-Sea and New Romney.

This whole section is dominated by the great shingle bank of Dungeness. Those who live near Chesil Beach in Dorset may disagree, but Dungeness is in fact the greatest shingle structure in the British Isles. It is odd to realise that Romney Marshes only exist because of the "fulls", as the locals call them, or the ridges of shingle. These "fulls" protected the land and let soil build up in the depressions behind them, otherwise Romney Marsh would be a salt lake. The Ness itself is moving eastward at the rate of about 10in a year. Don't let anyone tell you that the reason for the existence of the Ness (old English for headland) is that the shingle was carried by the flood tides which met here and dumped their loads – Kent tides are strong, but not strong enough to carry shingle about. Coast scientists say it is more likely that its pointed shape is due to wave action. Waves can move shingle, and those driven by long periods of south-westerlies are, it appears, to blame. Certainly it seems clear that the shingle is coming from the west.

From the Sussex border to Dungeness Point the land is mostly flat, and the shingle bank which protects the marshes is only about 3ft high. The Lydd firing ranges (marked on the chart) display red flags and lights from three 60ft high towers when firing is taking place. The range extends for a distance of 2 miles to seaward.

Looming over all at the Ness is the huge nuclear power station 167ft high. Just half a mile away to the east of the power station is Dungeness New Lighthouse – a black tower 141ft high with a white band and white top housing a permanently switched-on main light, at 50 54 48; 00 58 42E. This is not called the New Lighthouse for nothing. In fact there have been four lighthouses at Dungeness, the first erected in 1615. The second became redundant in 1792 when the shingle moved and left it behind. The third, built in 1904 and 143ft high, was blocked out by the new power station. This Old Lighthouse is still

The great Dungeness shingle bank dominates the coastline north of Dungeness Point.

there, 500yds to the west of the New Lighthouse, which was built in 1960 of pre-stressed concrete rings. Dive boat cox'ns will find it useful to know that getting the two lighthouses in line will give you a bearing of 274.5 degrees. They should also know that the nuclear power station's water intakes are marked by a lightbuoy 400yds offshore and 800yds south-south-west of Dungeness New Lighthouse. *Note* – Diver cox'ns should also be aware that the station's vertical water outlets in the seabed can create a disturbed sea 1000 to 1200yds offshore west of the New Lighthouse and that this turbulance can be a hazard to small craft.

The waters around the Ness become deep very close in and though tidal streams run close inshore they are weak. The bottom away from the shingle is fine sand over clay or mud.

There is a coastguard station just south of the Old Lighthouse and a coast-guard lookout at Lydd-on-Sea. An offshore lifeboat is stationed at Dungeness and an inshore boat at Littlestone-on-Sea.

Another landmark of this area, which from the sea can look like one long row of bungalows and between-the-wars holiday homes peering over the top of the shingle bank, is a square red brick tower at 50 59 00; 00 58 00E. This is at Littlestone. This mark can help divers to find the Roar Bank at 50 59 00; 01 01 00E. This shallow shoal has only 3m over it and runs parallel to the shore at Littlestone and about a mile off. There is another shallow bank closer to Dungeness. This is the Swallow Bank, with just 5m at best. There is a lot of foul ground round the Swallow. The inshore debris is mostly that of a Whale bridge unit which was intended to be part of the Mulberry harbours during the Normandy

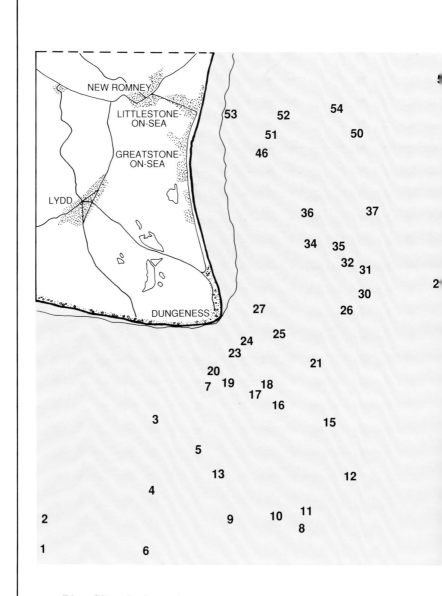

Dive Sites in Area 1

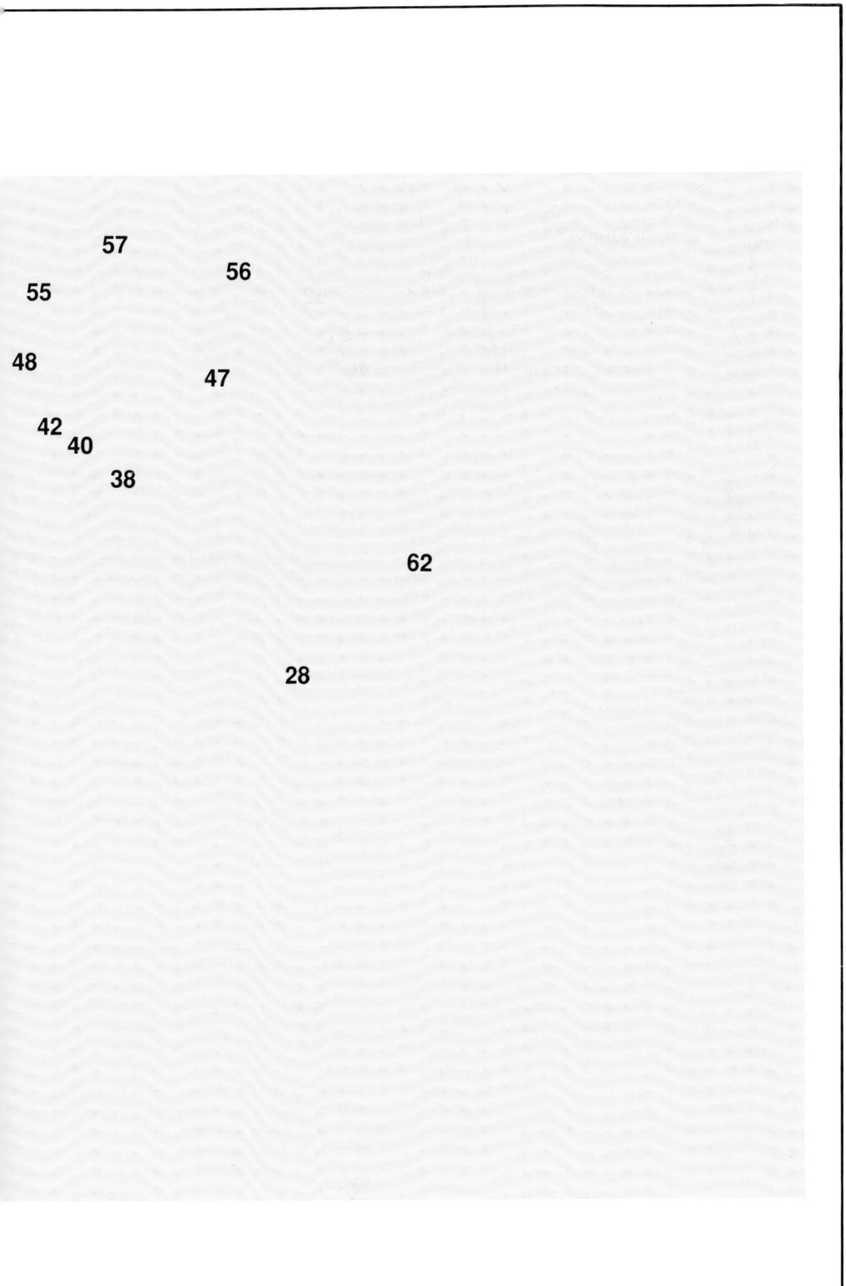

57

56

55

48

47

42
40

38

62

28

invasion, but grounded here and broke up. There are anchors and cables on the shallow outside of the Bank – and the wreck of the *Northfleet* is in the deeper water further out.

A general rule for wreck divers in this area is that the further west you go the siltier the wrecks. But there is no shortage of them. So many lie in the area from Dungeness to Folkestone that the Admiralty issues a general "health warning" to deep-draught vessels to avoid the area, which they say is "littered with wrecks". This is no doubt the reason why the Dungeness area is attracting more and more divers, many towing their inflatables from London and other parts of Southern England.

Launching sites

Though it is possible to tow a boat from Lydd through Denge Marsh to launch over the shingle on the far, or western, side of the nuclear power station, it is really a pointless exercise. Fairly simple launching can be made almost anywhere off the straight road running along the back of the shingle beach from Littlestone to Dungeness with such facilities close by as the Pilot Inn, with its big forecourt, near the Dungeness Lifeboat Station. Pilots used to land at the inn, having brought ships from London through the Straits. Launching over shingle can be hard work. However, things are easier at Littlestone where there is a wooden public launching ramp next door to the Inshore Rescue Boat station.

Above: wooden public slipway next to the RNLI station at Littlestone.

Diving sites

1 HMS Ghurka. This 880 ton destroyer (pictured above) was sunk by a mine in February, 1917 "off Dungeness". Divers on her today, at 50 50 48; 00 53 10E, will find that she has been extensively salvaged and explosives have been used in many places. Despite that, parts of her are intact and stand 8m proud in 30m.The *Ghurka* was built by Hawthorn Leslie and completed on April 29, 1907. She was 255ft long with a beam of 25.5 and a draught of 8. She was originally armed with three 12pdrs, but this was changed to five 12pdrs in 1911. She was built with two 18in torpedo tubes mounted one behind the other and just behind her three funnels so that they could be fired broadside. The 12pdrs were mounted with two at the bow, one each side of the bridge, and one firing over the stern. Her Parsons turbines could produce14,250hp.

The *Ghurka* was one of the 30-knotters of the Navy – indeed, she was known to reach 33 on occasions – but there was no question of that on the evening of February 8, 1917, for it was blowing hard, very dark, and the sea was heavy and tumbling. The mine exploded under her at 7.45pm "4 miles south-east of the Dungeness Buoy" and the long, thin ship started sinking immediately. A large number of the crew died in the explosion; most drowned before the nearest ship – the armed trawler *Highlander,* which was steaming down Channel – reached her after the explosion. By then only the tip of her bow was above water. The *Highlander* tried to launch her boat but it was swept away by the huge swells. Even so, the trawler managed to drag five men covered in oil from the icy sea.

Commander F.H.L. Lewin, the destroyer flotilla gunnery officer, was a passenger aboard the *Ghurka.* He was uninjured by the explosion and a very strong swimmer. He released one man from the tangled debris of the sinking bow and then refused to leave the water until he had helped four ratings to be rescued. He was later awarded the Stanhope gold medal for the bravest deed of the year. *Note* – Divers should remember that the *Ghurka* is a war grave under the Protection of Military Remains Act of 1986.

2 The Bottle Wreck is at 50 50 50; 00 53 33E. They say that hundreds of bottles were swept on shore after she sank. Perhaps the contents of those bottles are the reason why no-one seems to remember her name! Certainly this is the wreck of an old steamer, discovered by divers when freeing the nets of a local trawler. She is broken, about 350ft long and lying with her bows to the north-east. She is 9m proud at her highest point – the bow – in 32m.

3 UC-50. This minelaying submarine of the UC-II class, a 511 ton boat, 173ft long, had two bow tubes and one stern for which she carried seven torpedoes. She was able to lay 18 mines on each mission. Her deck gun was 8.8cm and was mounted just forward of the conning tower. She could dive in 30 seconds, but it was to prove not fast enough. Her last mission started from Bruges on January 7, 1918, when she set out into the open sea from Zeebrugge with orders to lay her mines in the Bay of Biscay. On February 4, presumably with her mission completed, she was spotted on the surface with her radio masts up at about 5.30am telling Bruges that she was to the west of the Dover Barrage and heading for home. The ship which saw her was the destroyer HMS *Zubian* which immediately went into top speed to ram the U-boat, and only just missed. But *UC-50* wasn't quite quick enough and the destroyer literally dropped a depth charge right on top of her. A fountain of oil shot into the air. *Zubian*, a "composite" destroyer made by joining the halves of the damaged destroyers *Nubian* and *Zulu* (Site 206), came round fast and sent three more charges down. They were set for 40ft and 80ft, but there seemed no need for them – more oil, cardboard and a Verey pistol cartridge came to the surface.

Kapitan-Leutnant R. Seuffer and his crew of 23 all died. Divers have found the boat at 50 52 48;00 57 08E. She is badly crushed amidships, but upright in 28m from which she is 6m proud.

4 HMS Gullfoss. An Admiralty trawler of 730 tons, which was completed in 1929. She was mined on March 9, 1941, and now lies at 50 51 30; 00 56 42E. She is upright and 9m proud in 28m.

5 Australier. A steamer of 3687 tons which was torpedoed on April 29, 1918. Five of her crew died. She is broken, but still 7m proud in 30m at 50 52 00; 00 58 06E.

6 Ceta. A Dutch motor vessel which sank after a collision on January 22, 1969. She is largely intact and is rated a good dive. She is 9m proud in a general depth of 30m at 50 50 06; 00 56 12E.

7 Unknown. This old steamer wreck at 50 53 09; 00 58 06E was first dived in 1970. She is upside-down but even so her keel is 10m proud of the seabed at 30m.

8 Aircraft. Judging by the length of the wreckage, this is probably a homeward bound Flying Fortress of World War Two, for the Fortress at 67ft is the nearest to the sonar measurement of its length as 66ft. Most German bombers were much smaller (Ju-88: 47ft; Heinkel 111K: 54 ft) and only the Wellington (64 ft) comes close as far as wartime British bombers are concerned, with the Lancaster too big at 69ft 6in. The highest point of the wreck at 50 50 35; 01 01 20E is at 27m above a seabed of 32m. This site is just inside the shipping lane.

9 Tokufuku Maru. This old Japanese steamer is well sunk into the sand-mud at 50 50 42; 00 59 25E. She was lost on March 25, 1924 and her masts and funnel were removed 17 days later because of the danger to shipping in the area. She lies almost exactly east-west with her bows towards Dover and is 154ft long, though she stands only 3m proud of the soft seabed at 31m. The wreck is just on the edge of the shipping lane.

10 Phoenix Units. Phoenix was the code name for the reinforced-concrete caissons which formed the walls of the Mulberry harbours which the Allies sank in position on the coast of France to supply the Invasion forces of 1944. Once the 213 units needed were built, they had to be parked – two-thirds were sunk between Selsey Bill and Bognor and the rest at Littlestone, near Dungeness. The Navy had great difficulty raising them when D-Day loomed (the wrong valves for pumping the water out of these giant concrete boats of egg-box construction was often to blame for this problem), but finally most of them were towed safely across the Channel. These caisson wrecks at 50 50 42; 01 00 54E are two of those which didn't make it. Their massive size means that they are of the A1 type of Phoenix – 204ft long and displacing 6044 tons each. Not surprisingly, divers have reported them as "huge – like tower-blocks of flats lying on their sides". Depth of these monsters: 21m on a seabed at 31m.

11 Bombardon. This was another Allied invention to stop storms breaking up the Mulberry harbours. Bombardon floating breakwaters were to shelter the harbour once sunk in position and break up waves before they reached it. Though no diving has been carried out on this site at 50 50 50; 01 01 34E, its length – 520ft – makes it likely that this is several sections of that breakwater. Depth: 23m in 33m.

12 Hosianna. The wreckage of this 56-ton ketch is at 50 51 34; 01 02 49E. She sank following a collision with the Dutch steamship *Zaandijk* while on passage from London to Barnstaple on May 7, 1926. Today the 98ft long wreck lies northeast to south-west with her bow down Channel. She is very broken and almost flush with the seabed at 32m.

13 Fulmar. Not much point in diving this old British steamer of 1698 tons at 50 51 48; 00 59 00E. So deeply is she sunk into the soft seabed that very little shows. She was carrying a general cargo when she sank after a collision on March 28, 1927, on her way from Liverpool to Rotterdam. She was 265ft long with a beam of 41ft. Depth is 32m.

14 The Oblongs. There are two of them, almost entirely under the seabed at 35m, and they are a massive 650ft and 568ft respectively. They lie parallel to each other with a gap of 160ft between them. This mystery is at 50 52 06; 01 07 04E. They may be more Invasion casualties, possibly Bombardons jack-knifed on each other, but no-one knows for sure.

15 Bobby. Was sunk after a collision with another steamer, the Dutch *Midsland,* on April 25, 1940. This Panamanian of 325ft, with a beam of 47, was in ballast and at anchor in thick fog at the time at 50 52 36; 01 02 41E. Built in 1905 at West Hartlepool and launched as the *Harmonic,* she had seven names in her long career. She was called *Eastbury* in 1927, and that was the name on her bell recovered by a diver in 1982. She is broken, but stands 12m proud of the seabed at 33m at her highest point and lies almost north-south. A deep scour runs for 100ft down her starboard side.

16 Excellence Pleske. This armed Danish merchantman of 2059 tons was torpedoed by Oberleutnant Johann Lohs in *UB-57* from a submerged position at 50 53 10; 01 00 46E. He noted in his log that he was not far from the Dungeness Lightship when he did so on March 31, 1918. He attacked the 275ft steamer, which had a beam of 37ft and a draught of 20, without warning while she was on her way from Bilbao to Middlesbrough with 2800 tons of iron ore. Thirteen of her crew went down with her, but the Captain was among the survivors.

It was third time unlucky for the *Pleske*. She had been attacked in the Mediterranean on July 30, 1917, by a different U-boat, but the torpedo missed. Another torpedo just missed her, again in the Mediterranean, on December 5, 1917. But Lohs, who had already sunk more than the 100,000 tons of shipping that made him an "ace", had more than his fair share of luck, and the cruise from Zeebrugge from March 15 to April 1 was no exception. Only two days before he sank the *Pleske,* he had sunk the *T. R. Thompson, a* much dived ship in Sussex waters.

The *Excellence Pleske* was launched by W.Gray and Co. in 1886 as the *Abeona.* A worn bell bearing this name was recovered in 1982 from the bow section, which stands 11m proud of the seabed at 31m. The *Pleske* has been swept and a section of her superstructure lies close to the north. Her bow points to the north and is the best preserved part of the wreck. Her engines – 203hp triple expansion, giving her a top speed of 9.5 knots – are uncovered, but silting is extensive.

17 Roode Zee. A long way from the warm waters of her name, this 468 ton Dutch tug lies at 50 53 12; 01 00 22E and is tangled up with the wreckage of another ship whose name is unknown. The tug was on her way to Portsmouth and was about 2 miles off Dungeness on April 24, 1944 when she was torpedoed by an E-boat. All of the crew of 15 plus a Trinity House pilot were lost. Her wreckage is in 32m and is 200yds west-south-west of the main wreckage of a much larger ship. (See site 18.)

18 Unknown. It is difficult to part this ship's wreckage from that of the *Roode Zee* (see site 17), but this unknown was at least 260ft long and the highest point of the wreckage is 12m proud of the seabed at 32m at 50 53 12; 01 00 32E. This is an old steamer and she is very broken and in two parts. Her boilers are clear to see and her bow suggests that she lies almost east-west.

19 Unknown, at 50 53 20; 00 59 15E. This wreck was first found during an Admiralty survey of 1973, standing 10m proud of a flat seabed at 33m. She was swept in 1975, which may account for the wreckage close by. No diving details, but she appears to be an old steamer of about 213ft long.

20 Sierra Bravia. This could be a Spanish motor vessel sunk in the 1960s, but divers have as yet produced no firm evidence that this vessel is the one lying at 50 53 38; 00 58 47E. They have found a ship, upright with her highest point – the stern – at 7m off a fairly flat sand-gravel seabed at 28m. Her holds have broken and her cargo appears to be railway lines.

21 Vittoria Claudia. This 2745 ton Italian steamer was carrying 4000 tons of iron ore and on her way from Bourgas to Hamburg on November 16, 1953 when

Lead ingots from the wreck of the SS Milbanke. Several hundred tons were raised.

she collided with the French motor-ship *Perou* of 7264 tons 2 miles south-east of Dungeness. The *Claudia* sank swiftly and though 5 survivors were picked up by the pilot cutter *Pelorus* 3 hours later, 20 other crewmen were lost. Built in 1905 by A.G. Neptun, she was operated by the Januense Societa di Navigazione. She was 292ft long and had a beam of 41. Today turbulence over the site will help to locate her at 50 53 46; 01 01 48E. Her bow is to the north-north-west and she has been swept. She is 11m proud. Depth to the seabed is 29m, though a 3m scour around her adds to that.

22 Unknown. A small wreck about 66ft long at 50 53 53; 01 06 51E, she is only 2m proud of the seabed at 31m, though this depth varies all round due to sandbanks. No diving information available.

23 Milbanke. This 1296 ton British steamer with 150hp steam engines was built in 1868 in Sunderland by the R.M. Hudson Co. Today, as a result of a collision with the steamer *Hankow* on July 28, 1874, off Dungeness at 1.30 in the morning when 14 of her crew died, she lies at 50 53 56; 00 59 39E. The 243ft long steamer had a beam of 31ft and a draught of 18 and was inward bound from Cartagena with a cargo of lead ingots. Depth is 23m on a seabed at 32m. She has been swept and salvage of her cargo over several years in the 1980s has altered her as well. She is broken in two almost exactly amidships. Her stern is intact, listing 25 degrees to port and about 9m proud. Most of her forward parts have collapsed. When divers first found her, her cargo of lead ingots was packed so close together that the divers could not get their fingers in between them. Each weighed 60kg and several hundred tons were recovered during salvage. The ingots were marked "F.RENTERO", "ORCHARDSON" and "Fm CONCEPCION MIGUEL Zj".

24 Unknown. She was carrying a cargo of granite chippings and appears to have been in collision. She lies at 50 54 09; 00 59 53E. Quite a number of tales have been told about this one – most exciting was that it was the wreck of a submarine with a seaplane on its deck – but when finally dived she turned out to be an old steamer, probably dating from before World War One, cut in two forward as though from a collision and with her cargo of big granite chippings spreading out around her. Both parts of the old ship lie close together on an even keel. She is about 230 feet long and the highest point is 8m proud of the 31m seabed, though there is a scour all around her taking the depth to 35m. She lies north-south.

25 Warship. This may be the wreck of an old destroyer, 200ft long, well sunk into the sand seabed at 31m, though the highest point is 6m proud. Position is 50 54 22; 01 00 37E. Sonar indicates that she is intact with a 2m scour around her, but there appears to be no diving information available.

26 Unknown. Very little to go on. A wreck 131ft long, lying more or less east-west at 50 54 49; 01 02 57E. Depth to seabed 30m, plus another 1m for the scour. The wreckage stands 4m proud.

27 Old steamer, name unknown, but the wooden deadeyes lying around suggest that she was rigged for sailing. Position is 50 54 51; 01 00 07E, depth 29m with her triple expansion engines and the bridge standing up 9m. The bridge is amidships of this early steamer of about 240ft long. From bridge to stern is intact and upright. Forward of the bridge is very broken. She lies almost exactly north-south with the bow to the north. Vis often exceeds 6m.

28 Unity. This 1091 ton armed steamer was owned by the Lancashire and Yorkshire Railway Co. She was built in 1902 by Murdoch and Murray with 302hp triple expansion engines which could give her 12 knots. Neither her speed nor her naval escort could save her, however. On May 2, 1918, Johann Lohs, in *UB-57,* had been waiting for a target from a position in the shadow of the Dungeness Lightship and on the dark edge of the area where the British searchlights lit up the whole Channel like daylight. Shortly after midnight, he spotted two steamers escorted by four gunships. He submerged and attacked one of the two steamers from periscope depth with one torpedo from his bow tubes. The *Unity*, which was carrying "ordnance" from Newhaven to Calais, sank swiftly, taking 12 of her crew down with her. The captain was among the survivors.
　　Today she lies 35m down on a sand seabed in the westbound traffic lane at 50 54 57; 01 13 36E with her bow towards the south-east. Her 247ft hull has been swept and is badly broken. Her boilers, amidships, are her highest point, 10m proud.

HMS Blackwater in 1908. She now lies in 27m with a huge gash in her port side.

29 HMS Blackwater. A 550 ton destroyer built by Laird for the "E" River Class and completed on July 25, 1903, she was in collision with the Bristol steamer *Hero* on April 6, 1909. Despite her armour, the 225ft long destroyer, which was only 23ft in the beam, was cut nearly in two when the *Hero* struck her amidships on her port side.

The collision came shortly after 11pm, as the Second Destroyer Flotilla was heading up Channel from Portland for the Firth of Forth and exercises. *Hero* was crossing the Channel and was obviously surprised to find herself amid a number of navy ships. In fact she just avoided a collision with another of the destroyers, before hitting *Blackwater*. Though *Hero's* bows were badly damaged, she was able to continue to port under her own steam. Commander M.D.E. Warren in *Blackwater* was much worse off. His ship was clearly sinking, but he took a tow from HMS *Forward*, which also took off most of the 63 officers and men of his crew. His ship, however, foundered about 5 miles from Dungeness. There were no casualties.

The *Blackwater* carried four 12-pounders (which replaced her five 6-pounders in 1907) and two torpedo tubes near her stern. She is now at 50 55 21; 01 06 10E and has been dived quite frequently. The diver on her today will be very aware of the collision damage – a huge gash and gap go almost completely through her from the port side amidships. Her telegraph has been recovered, but her two funnels are missing. Near the stern where her torpedo tubes were located there are the remains of two torpedoes, which should not be touched! Her nameplate has recently been recovered. Depth to her highest point near the bow is 18m. Depth to the seabed is 27m.

30 Cabo Espartel. On May 26, 1950, this 4000 ton Spanish steamer was in collision with the *Felspar* of Glasgow at 50 55 12; 01 03 43E and started sinking almost immediately; but there was still time for the Spanish crew to take to the boats. They were picked up by the *Fulham* of London and later transferred to the Dungeness lifeboat, which then guided the damaged *Felspar* to an anchorage in Sandwich Bay. The *Cabo Espartel* lies on a fine sand seabed at 33m with a 1m scour on both sides of her 348ft long hull. She has been swept and stands 12m proud.

31 Hydaspes. This very early steamer, fully rigged and of 2003 tons, sank in a few minutes after she was run down by another steamer, the *Centurion,* in dense fog 3 miles east-north-east of Dungeness on July 17, 1880. The 247ft *Hydaspes,* a British steamer, had engine trouble on her way from London to Melbourne and was under tow when the collision took place. She was carrying general cargo and is now at 50 55 26; 01 03 10E. The old steamer is, of course, very broken and deeply sunk into the sandy seabed at 28m. Even so she still stands 6m proud in places with a deep scour on both sides. She lies almost due north-south and is much rusted.

32 Jokai. This Austrian steamer of 1057 tons is at 50 55 46; 01 03 00E. She is there as the result of a collision with the steamer *Baron Ardrossan* on November 26, 1897, while on her way from Fiume (Rijeka, Yugoslavia) to Dunkirk via Rouen with 100 tons of general cargo. She was built in Barrow-in-Furness in 1882, 245ft long with a beam of 34. Today she is very broken in 29m with her boilers the highest point at 23m and her bow pointing almost due north. Divers recovered her named and dated bell in 1982.

33 City of Dresden. On January 19, 1907, this Irish steamer was on her way from Swansea to Hamburg with a cargo of copper ingots when she collided with another steamer and sank very quickly. All aboard were saved. The 1170 ton *City of Dresden* was 246ft long with a beam of 31 and a draught of 18. She had been built by Bowdler, Chaffer and Co. in 1876 and was owned by Palgrave, Murphy and Co. She had 164 hp compound engines. She now stands 9m proud of the seabed at 29m at 50 55 37; 01 08 01E with her bows to the south-west. She is very broken, and salvage of her cargo of copper ingots was completed in the late 1980s.

34 Samida. A Liberty ship which started life in California as *Annie Oakley* in September 1943. This 7219 ton all-welded steel ship was produced by Henry Kaiser and his team at the California Shipbuilding Corporation yard near Los Angeles – just one of at least 12 turned out every month during World War Two. This is a "Sam" ship – one of 200 Liberty ships loaned to Britain by the United States under lend-lease terms. All were given the prefix "Sam", not because they were gifts from "Uncle Sam", but because the British Ministry of War Transport liked to describe them as ships with the Superstructure Aft of Midships.

The *Annie Oakley* she was when she was laid down, but when she was launched she went into the water as the *Samida*. For 19 months she dodged everything that was thrown at her, but her convoy was found by *U-1023* on April 9, 1945 on the way from Antwerp to Barry Roads. Kapitanleutnant Heinrich Schroeteler, holder of the Knight's Cross for bravery, did not claim the *Samida* by name, but he reported firing a spread of three "LUT" torpedoes (lagen-unab-hangiger-torpedoes which ran on a zig-zag course) at a convoy on that day in that area and hearing two detonations. She sank quickly, but her crew of 43 and 7 gunners were all saved.

Today the *Samida* is at 50 56 14; 01 02 02E. She has been swept and is very

The 180ft frigate Northfleet: wrecked off Dungeness with a cargo of railway lines.

broken in 28m with her highest point, her boilers, some 9m proud. Her bow lies towards the shore.

35 Unknown, and likely to remain so, for this old steamer is now very broken and much covered by sand and silt at 50 56 19; 01 02 33E. She is about 230ft long, lies east-west and stands up only a little from the seabed at 30m.

36 Northfleet. This 180ft long frigate with a beam of 32ft was a fast ship, built in 1853 for the Far East trade in the Thames yards of John Patten at Northfleet. The 951 ton vessel had been hired by the Government to take emigrants to Tasmania to help build the island's railways. On January 22, 1873, many of the passengers were railway workmen with their families. As she lay at anchor that night off Dungeness, in her holds were 664 tons of railway lines, 100 tons of tin plate, 85 tons of salt, 2000 gallons of wines and spirits and 440 tons of general cargo. That cargo had gone as far as it was going to go – at 10.30pm the Spanish iron steamship *Murillo* came racing out of the dark and smashed a great hole in the *Northfleet's* starboard side amidships. The frigate started sinking at once and the passengers rushed the boats in panic. Captain Knowles tried to stop them with shots from his revolver but failed. Of the 370 people aboard, only 77 survived.

Today the *Northfleet* has the tip of her bowsprit buried in the mud of the Swallow Bank at 50 56 35; 01 01 13E in 28m and is remarkably intact. Though the bow is clear of the mud, the stern is buried in it. Midships on the port side the hull is a mass of plumose anemones, but on the starboard side the damage is concealed by the mud which is level with the top of the hull, swept there by strong ebb tides. The holds are open and can be entered, though the criss-crossed railway lines take up much of the space. Her bow is 4m clear of the mud and points to the west. She is still attached to the port anchor; the starboard anchor is at the bitts.

Tides are fierce on the Swallow Bank, and this and the mud make for generally poor visibility – although there are times when it is "gin".

The *Northfleet* is owned by members of Folkestone BSAC, who bought her from the Salvage Association in 1976.

37 Unknown, and so well sunk in that this one is difficult to find though she is at 50 56 46; 01 03 42 E. She is about 160ft long, lying exactly north-south in 25m, and standing only 4m exposed at the highest point.

38 Unknown. Was at one time thought to be the *Nunima* (see Site 48). This is an old steamer, which no-one seems to have put a name to. She lies at 50 56 50; 01 10 27E, and is very broken. Her holds are empty as though she was travelling in ballast. She stands 5m proud in 30m, but a scour on both sides takes that depth to 33m.

39 Naranco. This small Spanish steamer of 984 tons was built by Astilleros de Gijon in Northern Spain in 1920 with triple expansion engines. She was operated by Naviera Anjel Alvarez S.A. and was on her way, in thick fog, from Aviles to Rotterdam on August 23, 1959 when she was in collision with the m.v. *Goldstone.* The 213ft long steamer with a beam of 30ft sank in minutes, but there were 20 survivors. She now lies at 50 56 56;01 08 37E in 30m, is reasonably intact, and stands some 12m proud.

40 Sir Russell. A 1548 ton coasting collier carrying 2100 tons of coal, she was 6½ miles east-north-east of Dungeness when she was torpedoed by a German E-boat on August 11, 1941. The collier was 244ft long with a beam of 37 and was heading from Wear to Southampton. Her crew of 21 were all saved. Today she is at 50 57 15; 01 09 42E, standing 6m proud of the seabed at 30m, but a 3m scour adds to that. She lies east-west, has been swept, and is very broken amidships. Her bell was recovered by Bob Jessop, chairman of Folkestone BSAC, in April 1992.

41 Lizzonia. A 410 ton British motor-vessel, 142ft long with a beam of 27ft and a draught of 11, she sank within moments of colliding with the *Arctic Ocean* on March 16, 1961. The position of the *Lizzonia* is 50 57 20;01 08 01E. She is 7m proud of the 26m seabed, and she has been swept. She lies with her bows pointing towards the south-west.

42 Portslade. The day the *Portslade* was sunk – July 25, 1940 – was to be known afterwards as "Black Thursday". For this was the day when Convoy CW8, the eighth convoy of 23 colliers heading west, and laden with coal and coke for the factories of Southern England, was savaged by the bombers of the German air force from bases captured in France. Only 11 ships of CW8 passed Dungeness, and 3 of those were sunk further down Channel. In Kent waters lie the *Polgrange, Leo, Henry Moon, Corhaven* and the *Portslade,* which was carrying 1450 tons of coal from Sunderland and heading for Shoreham. She was hit by bombs from Junkers 87s, the dive bombers which had created such havoc during the German invasion of France. Her crew of 17 were all saved. She now lies at 50 57 25; 01 09 26E, with some of her cargo spilling out of her broken hull. Depth is 30m. She stands 6m proud with her bow to the north-east. There is a 1m scour around her.

43 Unknown, but a steamer at 50 57 29; 01 07 43E in 35m, from which she is charted as standing an amazing 17m proud despite having been swept. Divers on her say that the sweep must have missed a mast because that is the only reason for such a sounding. They report that this is a very old steamer, upright with hatches fore and aft, and about 290ft long. The scour of 3m is deepest at her stern, which lies to the west.

44 Unknown. At 50 57 35; 01 07 36E. Another old steamer nearly broken in two in 32m and standing 9m proud. Length about 290ft, nearly north-south with 4m scour.

45 De Fontaine. World War One had ended 5 days before, so this British collier of 1721 tons had little thought of trouble as she sailed in ballast from Dieppe to Sunderland. But mines have no knowledge of armistices, and it was a mine which sank her on November 16, 1918 at 50 57 41; 01 07 21E. She was 268ft long with a beam of 38ft and a draught of 17, built in 1907 by S.P. Austin and Son, and has been identified by her bell recovered by divers in 1982. She is 9m proud of the seabed at 30m, lying with her bow pointing almost due east, and is well broken, though the 4in gun still stands on her stern, as does the 12-pdr on her bow. Ammunition for the guns lies around them.

46 Empire Beatrice. Only 50ft of the stern is left of this 7046 ton British steamer, which was torpedoed by an E-boat when she was on her way to the Normandy Invasion on July 26, 1944 with a cargo of lorries and other heavy transport vehicles. She was badly damaged by the torpedo, but there were no casualties and her skipper managed to beach her near Greatstone. Here her stern was cut off and the rest of her was towed away and repaired. What was left was badly bashed about and the area is charted as "foul" in 3.8m. The position of the *Empire Beatrice* is 50 57 57; 01 00 20E.

47 Bricks ship. Was at one time thought to be the wreck of *UB-58,* which died in the dawn of March 10, 1918 when she dragged three British mines down with her as she dived to escape the attentions of a group of Dover Barrage patrol drifters; but recent diving has shown no sign of a sub at the site. What is there, at 50 58 06; 01 12 18E, is the remains of a ship which was clearly carrying a cargo of bricks. They are all in stacks amid the wreckage, which is about 187ft long and now has a 5m scour on both sides. She lies north-east to south-west with her bows to the south-west in a general depth of 25m.

48 Nunima. At 50 58 15; 01 08 44E. Divers have positively identified this 2938 ton steamer, which sank following a collision while on her way from Bilbao with a cargo of iron ore for Middlesbrough. She was 325ft long with a beam of 47 with 287hp triple expansion engines. She had been built by W.Gray and Co. in 1903. She was being operated by Trechmann Brothers at the time of her loss, on January 4, 1918. She is sitting upright on the seabed at 33m and is 12m proud. Her bows point up Channel and she is reasonably intact, though she has been swept.

49 Unknown. No clues to this steamer's identity, though she stands 10m proud in 28m. About 260ft long, she lies almost north-south at 50 58 20; 01 07 57E.

50 Charente. This old steamer, sunk on October 9, 1932, is at 50 58 27; 01 03 35E and has been swept to 14.6m in 22m. She is well broken but looks about 280ft long and lies exactly north-south.

51 Outsider. This is a 50 ton barge lost in a gale on January 4, 1922. She lies at 50 58 20; 01 07 57E in the mud of the Roar Bank and is well spread around after being dispersed in July 1925 to a depth of 5m.

52 Sparkling Star. A 48ft-long British MFV which foundered while under tow by the *Viking Princess,* another fishing vessel, on March 8, 1974. Her wreck is in just 6m on the Roar Bank at 50 58 40; 01 01 02E.

53 Phoenix unit. This is a B1 unit, 203ft long with a beam of 44ft, a concrete caisson intended to form part of the Mulberry Harbour at Arromanches in Normandy. She did not make it, however, and is now stranded and listing to east at 50 58 56; 00 59 06E near Littlestone. She dries about 6m. This unit is one of six smaller ones lost after being parked on the seabed at Littlestone. An official report on Mulberry, while pointing out that only one caisson was unable to be raised at the Bognor-Selsey Bill "storage" area, says that the Littlestone-Dungeness area "was bad on account of scour" and that was the reason for the six losses.

54 Whale Unit. Here is some more Invasion debris at 50 58 48; 01 02 42E. This whale unit – a pontoon to carry part of the floating roadway system in the Mulberry harbour – is well sunk into the mud in the East Road area.

55 Mrav. This 3870 ton Yugoslavian steamship, captained by Anta Begovic, collided in thick fog on April 29, 1936 with another steamer, the *Mari,* 5 miles south-east of Dungeness at 50 58 46;01 09 17E. The *Mrav* sank in 35 minutes – enough time for everyone to be saved. She was built in 1905 in Britain by R. Stephenson and Co. with 316hp triple expansion engines and was 341ft long with a beam of 47ft and a draught of 20. Salvage was carried out on her for 3 years in the 1960s. She lies with her bow towards the shore on her port side in 30m and divers should take special care, as her sides are collapsing inwards. There is a 3m scour on her eastern side.

56 Unknown. At 50 59 06; 01 12 42E. An old steamer 5m proud at 33m and about 240ft long, lying north-south. Hull is intact, though she has been swept.

57 Unknown. At 50 59 14; 01 10 27E. Not so much a wreck as a collection of debris from a wreck spread out over a large area and charted as "foul".

58 Unknown. At 50 59 08; 01 07 17E. This one was first dived in 1985, and proved to be a very old steamer, upright and in a very broken and poor state, though her bow and stern were still recognisable. Amidships she has collapsed, leaving the engine and boiler exposed. Her length was about 260ft and her highest point is some 8m above the seabed at 27m.

59 Aircraft. At 50 59 37; 01 06 29E. This wreckage, standing just 3m proud of the bottom at 24m, has not yet been identified, but Navy surveys suggest it may well be that of an aircraft.

60 Unknown. A very small, very broken, steamer. She sits upright at 51 00 00 ; 01 08 36E and stands about 6m proud of the bottom at 24m. So old is the wreck that the stern is just an iron skeleton. The top of this iron frame is the wreck's highest point, and the rest of the ship is sunk deep into the soft mud of the seabed. Even so, locals rate it a nice dive.

61 St.Cecilia. This 4411 ton British steamer was mined when on the way from Portland, USA, to London with a general cargo on March 26, 1916. She sank at 51 00 02; 01 11 14E some 4 miles east of the Folkestone Light Vessel, but all aboard were saved. Today she stands some 7m proud of the seabed at 25m and this 375ft long steamer is largely intact with her bows still pointing up Channel. Her bridge is still there, though her funnel has disappeared. There is easy access to the engine room. Visibility in the area can be brilliant, and divers have claimed to be able to see both bow and stern from the bridge!

62 UB-33. The Varne Bank route through the British minefields proved unlucky for Oberleutnant Franz Gregor and the 22 crew members of *UB-33* on April 11, 1918. He hit a mine at 50 56 00; 01 15 29E, and when Royal Navy divers went down to the wreck, they had to remove the body of Gregor from the conning tower before they could enter the control room in search of intelligence material. One of the divers hit the jackpot and surfaced with a steel box containing all the latest German codes and signals. Today the 121ft boat is largely intact at 32m on a sand-shingle bed and is upright with her main hatch still open. Her bows point up Channel.

The Inner Harbour (and slipway) at Folkestone.

AREA 2:

Hythe and Folkestone

Admiralty chart No.1892   **Ordnance Survey map 189**

This area runs from 51 00 00 eastwards to 51 05 20 and includes Dymchurch, Hythe, Sandgate and the port of Folkestone. The coastline is flat until the cliffs begin near Folkestone. There are six Martello towers between Dymchurch and Sandgate – a clear indication of how vulnerable this stretch was thought to be if Napoleon managed to launch his long-threatened invasion. The beach is studded with groynes to prevent erosion, but access to the sea is much complicated by the Hythe firing ranges (red flags when firing). Hythe has been planning a 600-berth marina for many years, but it is a long process. Among other things they need a Private Bill to allow them to breach the sea wall. This sea defence causes problems for those wanting to launch boats in the area. Hythe means "landing place" in old English, and it did once long ago possess a harbour – after all it was one of the original Cinque Ports. Hythe Flats is the name given to a shallow area close inshore between Hythe and Sandgate. Sandgate roads, off Sandgate Castle, have been known as a good anchoring ground for centuries. The seabed here is mud and clay in depths of 10-15m.

Launching sites

Shepway District Council – tel: 0303 850388 – maintains a number of launch sites, but the diver should be aware that many of them need keys to open the bar across them. Sites (with Ordnance Survey references in brackets) in this section are at:
St.Mary's Bay (094277). Concrete ramp with car park. Needs key.
Dymchurch (102293). Near Martello tower. Key needed.
Dymchurch (108300). Turn off main road by Pelican crossing. Wide concrete ramp. No key needed.
Dymchurch outskirts on A259 (114305). There is a steep ramp from the beach up to top of sea wall.
Hythe approaches (128319). Winding dirt road to top of sea wall.

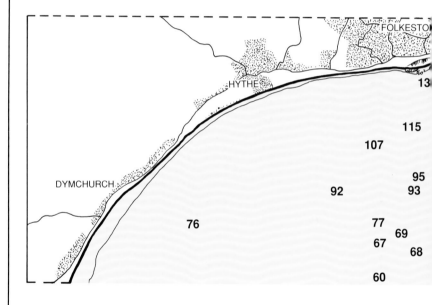

Dive Sites in Area 2

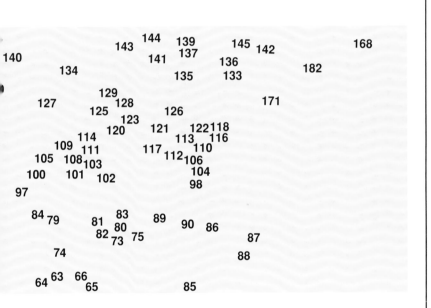

Hythe (163342). Entrance by narrow road beside Hythe and Saltwood Sailing Club. Steep wooden ramp. Permission required from club (Hythe 266343). The yacht club is also the home of Channel Divers (291 SAA).
Hythe (196349). Very steep off sea wall.

Folkestone Harbour

Channel 22   Folkestone Port Control: 0303 220544

This is a working port, not just a yacht haven. Roll-on, roll-off cross-Channel ferries use it and divers should take great care when entering or leaving. A blue flag at the mast at the head of the breakwater gives a 15 minute warning of the departure of one of these ferries and the port is then closed to all other traffic. The inner harbour dries completely at low water. The outer harbour formed by the 450yd long breakwater on the west is kept dredged to 4m. The modernistic Burstin Hotel which is set just back from the seafront is a good indication of the entrance to the harbour from the sea.

There are rocky ledges off Copt Point, which has East Cliff Martello tower above it, and there is the wreck of a lighter (see Site 140) just 800yds offshore. Mole Head Rocks run south-west from Copt Rocks nearly to the entrance of the inner harbour. In fact they come in so close that they are the site of several wrecks (see Site 138).

Folkestone Harbour is the home of the famous Folkestone Branch of the BSAC, who have led the way in Channel diving for many years. Their HQ is the Folkestone Yacht and Motor Boat Club in the narrow North Street at the back of the harbour, through the railway arches. (For details see appendix 4 at the back of this book.)

Visiting divers with their own boats can launch into the inner harbour by a concrete slip 3 hours either side of high water. The slip is located near the fish stalls – enter by the low arches. Permission required from the Harbourmaster, whose office is close to the slip. Divers wishing to leave their boats in the harbour overnight – on the mud – should ask the Harbourmaster's advice. Folkestone Yacht and Motor Boat Club do own some moorings near the bridge, but once again permission must be obtained from the Club. Ask Folkestone BSAC for advice.

Diving sites

63 Unknown. Is at 51 00 11; 01 14 19E. This 280ft long wreck lies only 125yds south of the wreck of the *Katharina Kolkmann* (see Site 64) across the tide in an east-west attitude, with a 2m deep scour on both sides. She stands 7m proud of the seabed at 27m.

64 Katharina Kolkmann. This 236ft long West German motor vessel was carrying 1500 tons of pig iron ingots from Wismar for Haulbowline when she collided in thick fog with the m.v. *Gannet* on March 29, 1965. She sank at 51 00 13; 01 14 19E about 5 miles south of Folkestone and stands 7m up from the seabed at 26m. She is flattened, though remaining upright with her bow intact. Her

The wide concrete public slipway at Dymchurch.

sides and bulkheads have collapsed, leaving some pig iron ingots in a great pile forward. The 1056 ton wreck lies across the tide with her bow to the shore.

65 Unknown. At 51 00 14; 01 15 33E is this 108ft long wreck standing only 3m proud in 27m. No diving information appears to be available.

66 Unknown. This one is a trawler or tug at 51 00 15; 01 15 23E, 110ft long and standing 7m proud in 25m with a scour of 4m. This seems to be an area of generally poor visibility at all times, but divers conclude from the big winching gear – all they could really see! – that this is a trawler or tug.

67 Grosser Kurfurst. The name means the Great Elector, who was ruler of the kingdom of Prussia. The *Grosser Kurfurst* was a great turreted ironclad of the German Navy, built in 1875. She weighed 6663 tons and was 370ft long with a beam of 52ft and a draught of 24. Her 850hp compound engines could push her along at 14 knots. On May 31, 1878, she was heading for service in Turkish waters as part of a German naval squadron. On a flat, smooth sea, the German ships headed down Channel past Folkestone. In the lead was the large ironclad *Konig Wilhelm,* the flagship of the squadron commander, Rear Admiral von Batsch. Slightly behind, not much more than a ship's length, and inshore of the leader, was the *Grosser Kurfurst* and much further astern was another turret ironclad, the *Preussen.* As they steamed majestically on, they suddenly found two sailing ships ahead of them, hauled to the wind on the port tack and so sailing right across their paths. The *Grosser Kurfurst* did the right thing, gave way, and porting her helm passed under the stern of the first merchantman, but the *Konig Wilhelm* tried first to cross the bows of the sailing ship and then changed her mind and porting her helm also passed under the stern of the merchantman.

41

The German ironclad Grosser Kurfurst goes down east of Dymchurch after a collision.

Meanwhile the *Grosser Kurfurst* had resumed her original course. The *Konig Wilhelm* now found herself tearing at her sister ship almost at right angles at six knots. The *Kurfust* increased speed to escape, but the helmsman of the *Wilhelm* lost his nerve and put the helm further to port instead of obeying an order to put it to starboard. The collision nearly knocked the *Kurfurst* completely over on her side and the *Wilhelm's* ram and bow ripped a gigantic hole in her. She keeled over. In 6 minutes she was gone, taking 284 of her officers and men with her. The *Konig Wilhelm* managed to limp on to Portsmouth, where she was docked.

Today the giant German ironclad lies at 51 00 47; 01 09 02E. The first divers down on her reported that she was in 15 fathoms and that she seemed to be almost split in two, with one part lying keel up and the other upright with part of a mast still standing. The divers put this twist down to her boilers exploding. The side of the upright section had a 20ft long hole torn in it.

Sport divers who have recently visited her all comment on the huge size of her plates – not surprising, as her turret plates were 10-in thick and the armour of her sides varied from 7-9in thick. The bow section is clearly upside down, as, it seems, is the rest of her, though much is sunk into the soft bottom. In fact the highest point of this huge wreck is only 10m proud in a general depth of 25m.

There is now a large hole where her ram used to be – it was raised long ago. Although it is possible to get into her or to swim under the plates, the constantly poor vis – it is very silty – makes this an extremely hazardous operation. Recoveries from the wreck are fairly modest – a porthole in 1992 and an anchor lamp with the glass intact. Divers should be warned – this is a dark site and only for the very experienced. (See also Site 99.)

68 Christianssund. This Danish steamer of 1017 tons is at 51 00 48; 01 09 47E as a result of hitting a mine on March 24, 1916. Divers found the 226ft long ship with a beam of 35ft, lying on her port side and intact although a good deal of her superstructure is collapsing down into the silty seabed. She was built in 1912 in Denmark by Helsingors Jernsk with 150hp triple expansion engines. Divers will see that the engines, like the bridge, are amidships. Depth is 27m due to a 1m deep scour. The highest point of her side is 9m proud.

69 Unknown, at 51 00 53; 01 09 27E. This is an old steamer, upright at 25m, 5m proud and about 370ft long.

70 Henry Moon. Another victim of "Black Thursday" and German dive bomber attacks on Convoy CW8 (see Site 42) , the *Henry Moon* was a 1091 ton collier carrying 1450 tons of coal from Burntisland in the Firth of Forth for Shoreham, on Thursday, July 25, 1940. She got just about level with Folkestone on her way down Channel, when despite her attempts to weave away, a bomb from the belly of a Ju-87 hit her, killing 1 man out of her crew of 16 and sending her to the bottom in 25m. Now she stands upright at 51 00 53; 01 11 50E with a big scour around her and with bow, bridge and stern 7m proud, though amidships she seems to be covering with sand and mud. This collier was built by William Pickersgill of Sunderland for the Brighton Electricity Undertaking. Her identity was confirmed by the discovery of her forecastle bell by Peter Weatherly of Folkestone BSAC, who found it wedged in the side of the bow.

71 Unknown, and looks likely to remain so for this old steamer at 51 00 57; 01 11 06E is sinking fast into the seabed and is now standing just 1m above it at 24m.

72 Unknown. Close to the previous wreck at 51 00 58; 01 11 15E is this 300ft long steamer lying up and down Channel, upright in 24m and 7m proud. She has been well swept and as a result divers have found that most of her superstructure is missing and her forward part is collapsing.

73 UB-78, or so she is if the evidence of the numbers stamped on the shafts of both her props is to be believed. Certainly this is the wreck of a U-boat, upright, but with her stern blown off at 51 01 01; 01 16 35E. There are torpedoes in her bow tubes. The discovery by local divers of the numbers on her props creates a

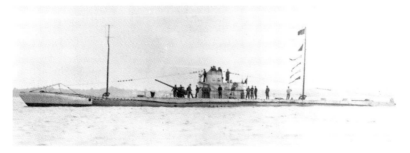

U-boat of the same class as UB-78 (see site 73).

HMS Brazen, a WWII vessel now lying upright in 30m with several guns in place.

new mystery. For *UB-78* commanded by Oberleutnant A. Stossberg is recorded as having been sunk by ramming by the steamer *Queen Alexandra* when she was transporting troops from Southampton to Cherbourg early in the morning of May 9, 1918. The U-boat was hit at 20 knots, just behind the conning tower, and sank at once. The position given was just north of Cherbourg and nowhere near this wreck. There seems little evidence that the U-boat rammed on May 9 was really *UB-78* and though a confirmed hit – 4 hours after the ramming there was a trail of oil and battery acid 7 miles long – the victim may have been another boat entirely. But which one? Lost in the Channel with graves unknown are *U-37, UB-36, UB-113, UB-108, UC-16* and *UC-18*.

74 Unknown at 51 01 02; 01 15 04E. No diving detail on this one, which from sounding does not seem big – about 95ft in length, standing 3m proud and lying almost north-south. She has been swept. Depth: 23m.

75 HMS Brazen. There were men at the guns still firing seconds before *Brazen* went down and though her anti-aircraft fire was responsible for three German dive bombers the Luftwaffe got her in the end on July 20, 1940, when she was escorting convoy CW7 through the Straits of Dover. The German bombers crippled her with a near-miss bomb under her, near the engine room, which broke her back. She sank while under tow. Casualties were light, with only one man dying from wounds after being taken off with the rest of the crew. The *Brazen* was one of nine "B"-class destroyers built in 1930-31. She entered Navy service on April 8, 1931. Her wartime crew numbered 175, her tonnage was 1360 and her length of 323ft had a beam of 32ft. Her armament was four 4.7in and two 2pdr anti-aircraft guns, together with eight 21in torpedo tubes. Her steam turbines developed 34,000hp and could push her along at 35 knots.

Today she lies at 51 01 05; 01 17 15E and stands 8m up from the bottom at 30m. She is upright and despite sweeping most of her superstructure is still in place. Her bow points to the north-west. One of her AA guns still points up to the sky, the other has fallen to the deck. Her heavier guns are all in place, but the German bombs seem to have blown her stern off – certainly you need to swim back over a sandbank amidships for some distance to find it and her two loaded torpedo tubes. Entry came be made behind the gun turrets, though it is silting. Bunks can still be seen and rows of gas masks and .303 ammunition is littered around.

76 Holland. This British steamer of 3828 tons, 350 ft long with a beam of 50, was built in 1906 by W.Doxford and Sons with 292hp triple expansion engines for Miller and Richards, who operated her as a collier. On November 24, 1916, she was carrying a full cargo of coal from the Tyne to St. Nazaire, when she was in collision off Hythe. She drifted in a sinking condition until she grounded at 51 01 07; 01 02 48E just a little over 3 miles from Hythe Church Tower. She was in shallow water and salvage operations and the weather soon broke her up. Most of what was left is now well sunk under mud and the depth over her is often only 1m.

77 Newcastle. Lies at 51 01 13; 01 09 00E where she was mined on October 10, 1915 when on her way home to London from Mauritius with a general cargo. She gave her position as "4 miles south-west of Folkestone Pier". The crew of this 3403 ton British steamer, 330ft long with a beam of 48ft, were all saved. First dived by amateurs in 1979, she was described as lying on a hard sand bottom on her port side. Her sides were in good condition and there seemed little sign of rust or break up. Her bow, pointing to the south-west, was in the same good condition, but extensively damaged by the mine blast. Her propeller was steel. Her superstructure was alongside, together with deck debris as a result of dispersal operations. She was positively identified by her bell. However, a diver only a few years later reported her now to be upside down. Sea bed is at 24m and her highest point is 6m proud.

78 Unknown. An intact but small wreck only about 55ft long and a mere 10ft wide, this is probably a small fishing vessel or yacht and has not been dived at 51 01 20; 01 11 23E. Depth is 23m and she stands just 2m high.

79 The Derry Steamer – that's what divers call this upright wreck at 51 01 25; 01 14 23E, but so far no-one has found her real name. Her nickname comes from a plate bearing the crest of the "Londonderry Steamer Company of Seaham Harbour" found near the bridge, which, together with the engine, is sited amidships. She was probably travelling in ballast at the time of her loss as both fore and aft holds are empty. Depth to her highest point is 17m and to the seabed 24m.

80 Unknown. The first of a cluster of wrecks. This one is at 51 01 27; 01 16 24E and is about 150ft long, a steamer half-buried in sand in 24m.

81 Unknown. Very close to the previous wreck, at 51 01 31; 01 14 01E. Another steamer also well sunk into the sand.

82 Unknown. Yet another ship, this time a wooden sailing vessel, whose wreckage appears to overlap the other two in the cluster, though little of her hull is to be seen at 51 01 31; 01 16 22E. Her cargo is clear – two large piles of railway lines in what were once her holds. A steel winch and big anchor lie nearby.

83 Steam tug. Lies just 70yds from the sailer of Site 82 at 51 01 32; 01 16 20E. No name yet, but this small steam tug, about 80ft long, sits upright in 24m. From the triple expansion engine's builder's plate we can guess that she was British as that bears the name of Richard Dunstan of Hessle on the Humber. Her bow, which is 5m proud, points straight down Channel.

84 Aircraft. Possibly another Flying Fortress, as the wreckage is about 70ft long, at 51 01 34; 01 13 51E. No diving information available. Depth: 24m.

85 Submarine. Unknown, but definitely German and an early model U-boat. That much can be told from the heavily encrusted depth gauge found lying amid the badly damaged wreckage at 51 00 06;01 18 43E. She has a very small conning tower and looks as though she has been rammed just forward of it. The submarine is cut almost cleanly there and is almost in two. She is 5m proud in 22m and more or less upright. Divers who have visited the wreck are convinced that this is one of the early Flanders Flotilla boats. (See Site 73).

86 HMS Drumtochty. Hired British trawler of 211 tons, 116ft long with a beam of 22ft and a draught of 12. Sank on January 29, 1918, after striking a mine off Dover laid by a German submarine. She is almost upright with a slight list to starboard, and is intact except for damage to the stern.She lies across the tide with her bows to the south-east in 27m at 51 01 18; 01 19 58E. The decking amidships is gone, making access easy. A number of cases of .303 ammunition can be seen and more is strewn around. She has been identified by her bell.
Note – There are large amounts of solid cylindrical explosives, grey-black, between 12-18in in length and 2-3in in diameter, scattered around the wreck. These are fillings for World War One shellcases. Trawlers were used to transport these fillings in quantity to larger ships during the War.They are still dangerous and divers should not bring them up.

87 UB-55. Kapitanleutnant Ralph Wenninger tried going through the Dover Barrage on the surface when outward bound from Zeebrugge in the dawn of April 22, 1918. At 4am, he spotted a trawler and a group of drifters ahead of him. *UB-55* crash-dived. At 12m his stern fouled two mine cables. They scraped

Depth gauge from the unidentified submarine off Dymchurch. (See site 85.)

along the hull before pulling the mines on to him. The double explosion opened the aft ballast tanks and the submarine plunged stern first to the seabed. She hit hard and nothing the crew could do would move her.

As the air grew hard and chlorine gas came off the batteries as the engine room flooded, some men panicked. Two chose to drown themselves, and two more shot themselves. They should have waited – Wenninger ordered the forward compartments to be flooded and then 20 men opened the hatches and shot upwards from 30m. Of these 20, only 5 were still alive when picked up 2 hours later by a naval drifter. One of those was Wenninger.

Today the sub is at 51 01 17; 01 19 53E. The 182ft long boat is lying with her stern to the east with a shallow scour on each side of her in the hard fine sand at 30m. She stands 5m proud and is upright.

88 Flachsee. Very, very close to the *UB-55* (see Site 87) and slightly to the south-east. This is the wreck of a 251ft German motor vessel of 1335 tons, which sank after a collision in fog with the *Canuk Trader* on February 12, 1963.

89 Unknown. A steamer well sunk in at 51 01 38; 01 18 19E. She stands 3m high in 26m. Was at one time thought to be the armed trawler HMS *Drumtochty*.

90 Granite ship. At 51 01 27; 01 18 42E. Though charted as an obstruction and not a wreck, divers have found the remains of a wooden ship here, which was clearly carrying granite blocks and boulders. Her cargo stands 2m high in 25m.

91 Shenandoah. This 3886 ton British steamer of 328ft long was mined on April 14, 1916 "1½ miles west from the Folkestone Gate". She was carrying general cargo and on her way from Halifax, Nova Scotia, to London. Two of her crew were killed in the explosion on her port side. Today she is at 51 01 47; 01 12 18E and that mine damage is very evident as she is upright and 7m proud of the seabed at 23m. Some salvage has been done as her propeller is missing and her four holds are open with some packing case fragments on the collapsed decking around the forward two holds.

92 Unknown. At 51 01 50; 01 07 33E. This one is small, about 85ft long, in 22m, and standing 3m proud.

93 UB-31. On May 2, 1918, just after 8am, Oberleutnant of the Reserve W. Braun was conning the 290 ton small attack boat *UB-31*, just 119ft long, through the minefields of the Dover Straits by periscope. He was heading home for Zeebrugge after a 16 day cruise, during which he had only managed to sink two sailing ships, one off the Lizard and the other north of Cherbourg. Coming through the Dover Barrage in daylight was a mistake – his periscope was spotted moving east-north-east by the Admiralty drifter *Lord Leitrim*. At the same time as he was spotted, Braun spotted the enemy. He crash-dived. *Lord Leitrim* dropped a depth charge into the surface tumult of his going. Oil and air bubbles came up. Another drifter (*Loyal Friend*) joined the hunt, and hovering overhead now was the British airship SSZ-29. The "blimp" called up another drifter, *Ocean Roamer*, which added another depth charge. This triggered a mine and *UB-31* and her crew of 2 officers and 21 men were finished. There were no survivors.

Today *UB-31* lies listing to port on the seabed at 22m at 51 02 03; 01 10 17E.

The 240ft-long cable-layer Monarch: upright and 6m proud in 24m of water.

She is intact, but there is no doubt about what killed Braun and his crew. It is clear from the large hole in the hull forward of the conning tower and the gun that a depth charge landed on her or exploded just above her forward gratings.

94 Sea Serpent. A British steamer of 902 tons, 225ft long with a beam of 33ft, she was on her way from Liverpool to Dunkirk when she hit a mine on March 23, 1916, 1 mile west of the Folkstone Gate. She sank so quickly that her captain and 13 of the crew died. Built in 1898 by A. McMillan and Son with a 78rhp triple expansion engine, she was loaded with corrugated iron sheets for building dugouts in the trenches of France. Today she is in 22m and standing 8m proud at 51 02 06; 01 11 28E. Although she is upright, all her superstructure is missing due to sweeping in 1960. Divers should be warned that her sides are eaten through by corrosion and big sections are liable to collapse. Her position is 300yds to the south-west of the Sandgate Buoy, where the seabed is hard sand.

95 Unknown, and so sunk in that little shows above the "bowl" she has created in the extremely soft seabed at 51 02 09; 01 10 12E. Depth: 20m.

96 Cleon. A British steam trawler of 266 tons, she was hired by the Admiralty for war service at the outbreak of World War One and lasted until February 1, 1918, when she ran into a mine laid by a German submarine near the Folkestone Gate buoy. Today she is very broken in 25m at 51 02 11; 01 11 18E.

97 Monarch. This is the second cable-layer to bear the name, but the first to be specially designed for the Post Office. Built of iron with one deck by David J. Dunlop of Port Glasgow in 1883, she cost over £40,000, was of 1122 tons gross, 240ft long with a beam of 33ft, carried a crew of 74 and could travel at 11 knots. She was launched into the Clyde at high water on August 21, 1883, and the champagne bottle was swung "gracefully" (according to the Glasgow Herald newspaper the next day) by Mrs. Anne Cunynghame, wife of Scotland's Surveyor-General. And *Monarch* performed well for the next 32 years until she struck a mine (laid by *UC-5*) on September 8, 1915 while going through the gate in the defence boom off Folkestone. An eyewitness said at the time that the ship started to settle down by the stern immediately after the explosion and in less than 3 minutes only the forecastle head was above water.

Divers have recovered a plate bearing her crest and her bell, damaged, has also been brought up from the wreck at 51 02 11; 01 13 44E. She is upright and after some dispersal stands 6m proud in 24m.

98 Laristan – and Denbighshire – and maybe a barge. Certainly a bit of a mystery at 51 02 17; 01 19 40E. A barge numbered *SCCR 382* was known to have sunk on August 28, 1942, after springing a leak while under tow of the tug *Goliath*. In 1961 a drift sweep revealed something much bigger than a barge at the position. Later soundings revealed two wrecks. One is 230ft long and the other, parallel to it and only 32ft away, is over 300ft long. The smaller one, which was thought to be *SCCR 382*, stands only 5m off the bottom, but the larger one is a good 12m proud of the seabed at 26m. More recent diving has revealed that the larger wreck is that of the *Laristan*, a cargo steamer of 2134 tons, 290ft long with a beam of 42, built in 1896 by W.Gray and Co. She was in collision with the steamer *Crimea* on October 22, 1899, while she was travelling from Bona to Rotterdam with a cargo of iron ore. She has been identified by her bell. Today she sits upright with her bridge and 218hp triple expansion engines amidships. Diving the other wreck showed that she was in fact a schooner called *Denbighshire* – according to the name on her bell – and her sinking about 1889.

99 Unknown. At 51 02 18; 01 12 43E. At one time this was thought to be the position of the *Grosser Kurfurst*, but as diving has identified Site 67 as that of the great German ironclad, this is now an "unknown", showing only 2m above the mud at 22m.

100 Kielce. This Polish ammunition ship of 1896 tons was sunk in 1915 just a mile south-west of the Northern Light Vessel marking the gateway of the swept Dover Channel. She was carrying aircraft bombs, large calibre shells and small arms ammunition. One report says that she was on charter to the United States Maritime Administration at the time, which makes her role in the War at that time rather confusing. She was dispersed in 1963 and salvage operations have been carried out. Her wreckage is now scattered over a large area of seabed some 120yds by 80yds in 23m at 51 02 19; 01 13 46E.

101 Barracuda. This 24ft fishing vessel sank on May 2, 1979 in 23m of water at 51 02 20; 01 15 12E. No diving information available.

102 Kadrv. A lighter of 64ft long with a beam of 21ft, which sank while under tow of the tug *Quaysider* on August 26, 1984 at 51 02 24; 01 15 57E. She stands 3m proud in 25m and some salvage work has been carried out.

103 HMS Carlton. Described in one set of records as an Admiralty-hired trawler of 267 tons, 180ft long, and in others as a steam tug with the same dimensions,

Pomerania – a big liner now rated by divers as one of the best wrecks in the area.

this wreck lies at 51 02 35; 01 15 44E. She was finally firmly identified as a steam tug built in 1907 by a diver who brought up her builder's plate in 1982. Now she lies in 28m and her stern is 7m proud. The fact that she was mined on February 21, 1916, is clear. A large section of her bow is missing, but she is upright with cabin intact. The wheelhouse is nowhere to be seen.

104 Falmouth III. At 51 02 38; 01 19 01E. One of the three ships sunk by four mines which were laid by the German submarine minelayer *UC-5*. It was commanded by Oberleutnant Herbert Pustkuchen. On the night of November 16-17, 1915, he laid the 4 out of his cargo of 12 as Barrage 20A (numbered according to the total number of minefields laid by the U-boats of the Flanders Flotilla based in Bruges) and almost as an extension of the line of Dover Harbour's western arm. The *Falmouth* was a minesweeper, a converted hired trawler of 198 tons, and on November 19 she was commanded by Lieut. H. Beadle, DSC, who was showing two young RNR officers the ropes. One of them, Sub-Lieut. W.A. McIntosh was killed in the sinking, which put the wreck right on top of that of the *Anglia* (see Site 122) and she stayed there for several days until a gale shook her off. Today she is well-broken and much of her is level with the sand-mud seabed at 24m, though the port side and the boiler still stand up nearly 5m.

105 Unknown, at 51 02 40; 01 14 10E. A steamer standing 4m proud in 23m, lying east-west, and about 170ft long. Diving details required.

106 Pomerania. A big liner, built in 1873 by J. Caird and Co. for the Hamburg-Amerika Line, she lies at 51 02 43; 01 18 48E and is 6m proud in 25m. She lies east-west on her port side with her bows to the east. Some divers rate her as one of the best dives in the area.

Commanded by Captain Schwensen, the liner, which was 360ft long with a beam of 40ft, sailed from New York bound for Hamburg on November 14, 1878. When she called at Plymouth, she landed passengers and mail for England, and also 7500 dollars worth of gold. When she continued her voyage she was carrying 109 passengers and 111 crew. Just before midnight on Monday, November 25, off the coast between Folkestone and Dover, she was travelling at her top speed of 14 knots when she was struck on the starboard side nearly amidships by the iron-hulled barque of 1100 tons, the *Moel Eilian,* commanded by Captain Pritchard. The *Pomerania* was badly holed and started filling. Four out of her nine lifeboats were smashed by the collision; the other five got away, but one was so overloaded that it capsized and many of those aboard drowned. The *Moel Eilian* was so badly damaged that she could not help and headed for Dover, which she reached just in time. The *Pomerania's* distress signals brought the steamer *Glengarry* to her aid and Captain Hogg and his men saved a large number of people. The liner took 20 minutes to sink and this delay lured some passengers to go below for their valuables. They went down with her when she suddenly sank. In all 48 passengers and crew were lost. Captain Schwensen went down with his ship, but came to the surface and was picked up by another rescue craft.

The *Pomerania* today is well broken, but parts of her wooden deck are still intact. A recent dive found some of the passengers' valuables – 25 silver and gold coins. The silver coins were marked "United States Trade Dollar, 420 grains, 900 fine" and dated 1877. The gold coins were 20 and 50 mark pieces. Much of her cargo appears to be clock mechanisms in boxes and her sails have been found neatly rolled in her sail lockers.

107 Obstruction, at 51 02 45; 01 08 34E. No one knows what this one is – possibly some more Invasion debris. It is 32ft square and stands 2m proud in 21m.

108 Collier, name unknown. This 120ft long wreck has coal all round her at 51 02 49; 01 15 01E. Divers have found her to have two holds forward and two aft in her 25ft beam. Her bow is broken off about 20ft from the prow and this section is lying on its port side. The rest of her is upright, but sweeping in 1961 has flattened her superstructure. Her engine is amidships. Depth is 23m.

109 Trawler. Upright on bottom at 24 m at 51 02 53; 01 14 46E. Has large A-frames fore and aft and her superstructure is largely intact. Stands 7m proud. She was thought at one time to be the *Carlton* (see Site 103).

110 Lusitania. Another victim of *UC-5's* four-mine field (see Sites 104 and 122), the *Lusitania* was a British steamer of 1834 tons, 270ft long with a beam of 39ft, and was basically a collier, though at the time of her sinking she was carrying Government stores and general cargo from London to Lisbon. When her captain heard the explosion of the mine which sank the *Anglia* at 12.30pm on November 17, 1915, he turned back to her assistance – and ran into the minefield himself. Though his ship turned turtle and floated keel up for some time before sinking, the captain and all his crew were saved. Now she is at 51 02 55; 01 19 05E and upright again in 24m. Near her boiler she is 8m proud, though her superstructure and decks have collapsed inwards. Her bow is to the north and there is a 1m scour in places around her. There is no doubt about her identity – divers have recovered her maker's plate. During survey operations a very small wreck was found 200yds to the east of her, but has not yet been identified.

111 South Folkestone Light Vessel. Designated as Light Vessel No 75, she was bombed and strafed by German aircraft and sank in the sunlight of August 14, 1940. Two of the crew of seven from the 130ft long vessel were killed in the attack. Today she lies on her side at 51 02 56; 01 15 46E. She looks intact though her hull is clearly bulletholed. The big lamp is missing. Depth is 22m, though a scour adds nearly another 2m and her highest point is 6m proud of the seabed.

112 Unknown, at 51 02 56;01 19 16E. A steamer lying north-south with her bow to the north in 26m. She is upright, but much of the superstructure and decking has collapsed inward. Height is 6m.

113 Unknowns. There appear to be at least two wrecks here tangled together at 51 03 00; 01 19 21E. One is well sunk in with only 2m above the mud in 28m, the other, or others, appear small – about 100ft long – and are slightly to the south-west.

114 Unknown. A 230ft steamer with the engine amidships lying almost due north-south at 51 03 04; 01 15 20E. Depth is 28m, but a scour brings that to 30m from which she sits up nearly 8m.

115 The Slate wreck. This wooden ship with iron ribs doesn't stand much above the seabed at 51 03 05; 01 09 57E, but her cargo does. At one time this site was thought to be a rock, but diving proved it to be the slabs of slate in her cargo which gave that impression. The stacked slate is 3m proud of the seabed at 20m.

116 Landing craft. Another pre-Invasion casualty, this landing craft (Infantry) at 51 03 06; 01 19 51E was to be used to put troops on the beaches, but sank before the assault. She is small, about 65ft long, and stands 2m proud of the seabed at 26m. She was first dived in 1984.

117 Cement wreck – that of a small steamer with engine at the stern, upright at 51 03 09; 01 17 50E. She is about 196ft long and stands 6m proud at 22m, with her bow to the west. Divers call her the cement wreck because of her cargo – blocks of cement looking like the bags which once held it before the sea solidified them.

118 Unknowns. Two wrecks without names lie at 51 03 09; 01 19 47E in 26m. One seems to have her bow to the south-west and parts stand 5m off the seabed. The other, more broken, is slightly to the south-east and small at about 80ft. No diving information available.

119 Oakby. A 1976 ton steamer which lies at 51 03 13; 01 11 36E, but is hardly recognisable as a ship, were it not for her boiler and parts of the steering gear at the stern. She was once upright, but is now broken over a wide area in 22m. First dived in the mid-80s, she is regarded as a good dive for novices. The *Oakby* was torpedoed in the afternoon of February 22, 1915, when two miles east of the Royal Sovereign Light Vessel travelling from London to Cardiff in ballast. She didn't sink then, but at 6am the next day, when under tow for Dover.

Boats pick up survivors as the WWI hospital ship Anglia goes down. (See site 122.)

120 Submarine. This one sits upright, 4m proud, with her gun *in situ,* but her conning tower broken off and her bow and outer hull forward badly damaged in 23m at 51 03 15; 01 16 38E. She has been dived and is a U-boat. But which? (See Site 73.) Her gun, which was ahead of the conning tower position, has been salvaged. One suggestion is that she was one of the U-boats surrendered at the end of World War One and was under tow to the breakers when she sank in April 1919, but there is no confirmation of this.

121 Unknown. This 250ft long steamer with a beam of 33ft is at 51 03 15; 01 18 09E. She stands 8m proud and is upright but in a poor state with all her superstructure collapsing in on herself. Her bow points to the south-west and is broken about 30ft back from her prow, so much so that most of the bow section is almost level with the seabed at 25m. Amidships her engines provide the highest point of the wreck.

122 Anglia. A twin-screw ship owned by the London and North-Western Railway Co. before being taken over as an auxiliary hospital ship. This was the worst casualty of the minefield laid by *UC-5* on November 16-17, 1915 (see Sites 104 and 110), for the *Anglia* was a hospital ship packed with victims of the trench warfare who had got their "Blighty One" and were on their way home from France for treatment in hospitals in Britain. There were 366 wounded aboard and most of the seriously wounded were on bunks in the two front wards of the ship. They were the first to suffer when, at 12.30pm on November 17, with the white cliffs of Folkestone in sight, the *Anglia* hit a mine which exploded just forward of the bridge on the port side. Within moments the hospital ship was down by the bow and listing to port.

Built in Dumbarton in 1900 by W. Denny and Brothers, she was registered in Dublin. She was a fast ship of 1862 tons, with 424hp triple expansion engines, giving her a top speed of 21 knots. On this run, the 329ft long ship, which had a

Above left: vented porthole from the 329-ft long Anglia (above right).

beam of 39ft and a draught of 16, was commanded by Captain Lionel John Manning. The explosion blew him from bridge to lower deck, but he combined with his Chief Officer to get the port side boats away. Rescue ships closed on the sinking *Anglia,* whose propellers went on spinning madly in the air as her stern rose higher and higher. Finally she almost righted herself before plunging under the surface completely. From explosion to sinking had taken 20 minutes.In all, 129 people died in the tragedy.

The *Anglia* was the first hospital ship to be sunk during World War One, and lies slightly to the north of the other two victims of the four mines in the small field laid by *UC-5* the previous night. She is at 51 03 21; 01 19 14E in 25m with her bow to the north. Though well sunk into the sand-mud, she is all there, even if sweeping in 1961 didn't help. Some parts of the central portion stand up to 6m proud. Divers in 1983 found dinner plates marked with "London and North West Railway Co.", confirming that the wreck is that of the *Anglia*. Divers should not enter any remaining sections or interfere with the wreck as it is very much a war grave.

123 Unknown. In June 1919 a buoy was put on this wreck at 51 03 33; 01 16 43E, believing it to be a German submarine. In 1922, the buoy was taken away without saying why. In later years she was sounded as about 180ft long, standing 6m up from the bottom in 22m. Those dimensions led German sources to think, in 1971, that this might possibly be *UB-113,* still missing after operations in the Channel in September 1918. However, all these theories were confounded when she was dived in 1982 and turned out to be the upright wreck of an old cargo steamer.

124 Swiss aircraft. This small aircraft lies in two parts at 51 03 34; 01 11 11E. She ditched in the sea after running out of fuel on a flight from Geneva to London in June 1954. Has been dived and the wings, separated but each with an engine attached, located. The fuselage of the Swissair Convair has not yet been found. Depth: 20m.

125 Leicester. A British "store carrier" of 1001 tons, this 240ft steamer with a beam of 32 was coming from Portsmouth to Cromarty with a general cargo for her owners, the Great Central Railway Co., when she was mined at 51 03 34; 01 16 03E on February 12, 1916. Seventeen men died when the old ship – built in 1891 – sank swiftly 2½ miles south-east by east of Folkestone Pier. Today, due to dispersal and salvage operations, her wreckage is broken in two at 21m. Both her bridge and forecastle bells have been recovered by divers. The smaller, the bridge bell, was found to be damaged, possibly by the mine explosion. The *Leicester* was certainly carrying stores – divers have found rows of plates, marked with crown or anchor, some in boxes bearing the letters "W.R." or "W.O", hundreds of silver plated spoons and forks (but, to their annoyance, no knives!), soup tureens, boxes of jars of pickles – mostly cauliflower florets – and jars of drinking chocolate.

126 Unknown. At 51 03 34; 01 18 21E. A small steamer about 60ft long, well sunk into the mud bed at 24m and only 2m proud. No diving information available.

127 UB-109. Though the Admiralty think that the submarine at 51 03 41; 01 14 14E may possibly be *UB-31* (see Site 93), I am convinced that this is really *UB-109*, commanded by the veteran Kapitanleutnant Ramien, who at the end of July 1918 slipped through the gap in the Dover Barrage minefields off Folkestone, known as the Folkestone Gate, which was there to let Allied shipping through in safety. Once through, Ramien set off to sink shipping around the Azores. While he was away, the British realised that the Gate was a weak spot in their defences and planted shore-controlled mines and hydrophones in it, linking them all to a listening station high on Shakespeare Cliff. The Germans soon realised that the Gate was mined and radioed a warning to all U-boats. Ramien didn't hear it – he was out of range because he had ordered his long-distance aerials to be taken off his boat as he felt they made him top-heavy! He decided to slip back through the Folkestone Gate, at the maximum depth at which he could use his periscope – with his keel 35ft below the surface. As he prepared to go through he saw the Navy trawler *St. Germain* on traffic control duty at the Gate and decided to go inside her on the landward side. This sent him straight over the hydrophones.

UB-109 was a 640 ton boat, 182ft long with a beam of 19ft. She normally carried a crew of 34. However, some reports say that 38 men were aboard just after 3am on August 29 when Ramien started his run. Almost immediately the listening station locked on to him. For 17 minutes in the station on Shakespeare Cliff they listened and waited. Then the needle of the galvanometer swung hard over as Ramien crossed the line of mines in the Gate. A forefinger stabbed down on a button and in the huge explosion which followed only Ramien, his navigator and six men reached the surface. The wreck was buoyed and shackled by the Navy before the morning was over. The first divers inside her collected valuable material from the control room and the "WT cabinet" for the Navy's intelligence department.

The U-boat has been dived frequently since. She is in 22m and the damaged stern has now parted from the forepart. They lie about 30ft apart and even so part of the stern appears to have disappeared entirely. If that means the loss of her propellers, the final proof of her identity (her number stamped on the shaft of the props) will be difficult to discover. However, the experienced Channel diver Tim Bennetto tells me that when he first saw her in 1983 she had her periscope extended some 12ft above the conning tower hatch, which was open. The gun and her props were still in position. Later diving showed that on the shank of one prop was the number *UB-109* and on the other *UB-104*. This is confusing, as *UB-104* is thought to have been lost near Fair Isle in the Orkneys!

128 Unknown. At 51 03 44; 01 16 37E. A steamer lying east-west and upright, but broken with the highest point some 3m off the seabed at 21m.

129 Unknown. Very small and very well sunken into the seabed at 51 03 56; 01 16 26E in 20m. No diving information available.

130 UC-77 is at 51 03 59; 01 12 33E, all because of the inexperience of her new commander, Oberleutnant J. Ries. *UC-77,* a 493 ton boat, 166ft long with a beam of 17ft, carried 18 mines on each mission and after she had laid those could sink more ships with 7 torpedoes and her 3.4in. gun. From her launch in 1917 until Ries took command, she had sunk by mines, gun and torpedo some 32 ships totalling 49,062 tons of Allied shipping, and was considered by her crew to be a lucky boat. Luck couldn't cope with the lack of precautions her new commander took before attempting to run the Dover Barrage in the afternoon of July 10, 1918. Behind him when he dived to start his run submerged, he left an unmistakeable trail of air-bubbles and leaking oil. Two Dover Patrol drifters, *Kessingland* and *Golden Gain* spotted it and following it to its source, dropped four depth charges. Three more explosions followed – probably as a result of some of the U-boat's mines detonating – and great gouts of oil burst up to the surface. There were no survivors.

Today she lies almost exactly north-south and is charted as 20.3m in 22m. She was relocated by divers during a survey of cross-Channel electricity cables for the Central Electricity Generating Board. She is well sunk in to the soft seabed and shows clear signs of the depth charge and mine explosions.

131 Benvenue. The hurricane which struck Kent on Wednesday, November 11, 1891, caused widespread damage all around the coasts of Britain. Ships at sea were in big trouble. The fully-rigged 2033 ton *Benvenue* was one of them. The 289ft long sailing ship with a beam of 42ft and a draught of 24 had left London the morning before with general cargo for Sydney, Australia and was towed down Channel by a London tug. On the Wednesday when she reached South Foreland the wind became a gale from the south-west. At 9pm, when she was off Sandgate, that gale became a hurricane and the sailing ship became unmanageable. She dropped both anchors, but they didn't hold and she drifted towards the shore at Seabrook. A few hundred yards from the beach she struck and started to sink at once. The crew took to the rigging. They could see people on shore trying to launch the lifeboat – and failing because of the boiling surf.The lifeboatmen tried again and one of the crew drowned when she capsized. Further along the coast a French schooner, the *Eider,* was dashed against the Seabrook sea wall; four men were saved from that though the Captain, his wife and nephew drowned. Then rockets were fired from the shore to the *Benvenue* and though they actually struck the men in the rigging, none of the lines could be secured. On the third attempt the lifeboat was finally launched and 27 men were taken off from the rigging after 16 hours and landed at Folkestone. The cox'n of the lifeboat, Lawrence Hennessey, was awarded the Albert Medal and his deputy the silver medal of the RNLI. Five of the crew of the *Benvenue,* including her captain,

Fighting for life during the wrecking of the Benvenue in 1891. (See site 131.)

drowned before the lifeboat could reach them. Queen Victoria authorised a special medal to be struck for each member of the lifeboat crew.

Today the *Benvenue* is at 51 04 05; 01 08 10E and she and her cargo of bed-
steads, fireplaces, bottles of beer, rum, wine and jars of herrings, jam, and other

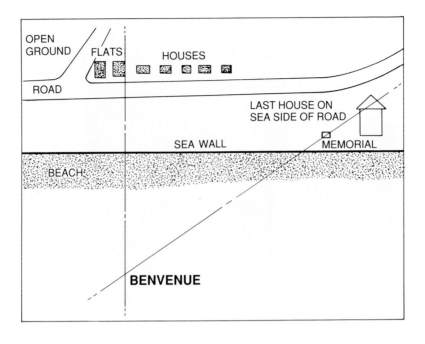

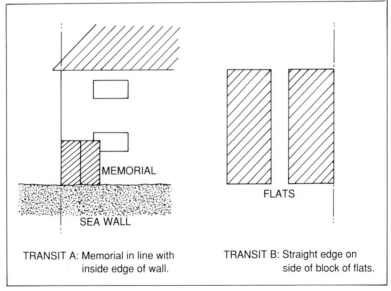

TRANSIT A: Memorial in line with inside edge of wall.

TRANSIT B: Straight edge on side of block of flats.

Marks for the wreck of the Benvenue (site 131).

The 960-ton collier Pulborough: sunk by German bombers 2½ miles SE of Dover Pier.

items the Australian settlers would have found useful are widely scattered and sunk deep in the fine sand where she struck some 300yds offshore. Depth: 9m, and surprisingly, one section of wreckage still stands nearly 3m proud.

132 Dorothy J. A 32ft fishing vessel which sank at 51 04 12; 01 10 54E on February 24, 1990. Position is approximate as she was being carried to the north-east as she was sinking. Depth is 8m. Not yet located by divers.

133 Pulborough. A British collier of 960 tons, laden with 1360 tons of coal from the Tyne for the power station at Shoreham. She was attacked and sunk by German bombers on July 20, 1940, when she was about 2½ miles south-east of Dover pier. All her crew of 17 were saved. It was the start of the German Air Force's attempt to close the Channel to Allied shipping and so cut off the electricity supply to the War factories of Southern England. At 51 04 17; 01 20 14E, she lies across Channel in 25m, is upright and 7m proud, but has no scour around her.

134 Norman. This is a 100ft long barge at 51 04 21;01 14 51E, sunk on October 7, 1944, in 22m and standing 4m proud.

135 Leo. Another collier victim of dive bombers on "Black Thursday", July 25, 1940 (see Site 42). In Convoy CW8 on that day *Leo* was placed astern of another collier called the *Tamworth*. The Merchant Navy gunner on the *Tamworth* was John Gallagher. He described the end of the *Leo* like this: "At 4pm the klaxon for action stations blared throughout the ship and out across the water to our mates. Astern the *Leo* was already closed up. We waved to the gunners on the *Leo*. They waved back. Then there was the howl of dive bombers. I fired our stern 12-pounder at them. Walls of spray burst up around us. Suddenly four Junkers 87s came rocketing over the waves towards us on the starboard quarter, machine guns going and hitting. My gun wouldn't bear but Eric Speakman on the bridge with our twin Lewis guns was grinning his head off as he blazed away at them. Then the planes were over us and gone. I looked astern. There was no *Leo* of Hull steadily shouldering the waves away behind us. There was just the bottom of a ship rolling in the water, with two men standing on the propeller shaft as the up-turned hull drifted astern of the convoy...". Moments later Gallagher got a shot in and blew another Ju87 to pieces. And then *Tamworth* was hit, but was towed in to Dover.

Leo, oddly for a ship with such a British name, had been built in 1908 by the German Stettiner Oderwerke. She was 226ft long, of 1140 tons, with a beam of 34ft and draught of 14ft and had 128hp triple expansion steam engines. At the time of her loss she was carrying 1536 tons of coal from Seaham to Portsmouth and was owned by Ellerman's Wilson Line. Though the *Leo* was upside down when seen by the *Tamworth*, only 6 of her crew of 27 were killed. Today she is at 51 04 22; 01 19 02E, in 32m on a steeply-sloping seabed on her side and only 3m clear of the sand which is rolling down on her.

136 Unknown. At 51 04 40; 01 20 28E. An old steamer 260ft long in 30m standing 6m proud and lying up and down Channel.

137 Unknown, but it has been suggested that this could be *Angelus* (see Site 139) or *Maloja* (see Site 141) . Certainly this is the wreck of a steamship at 51 04 43; 01 18 58E. Depth is 27m and she stands nearly 9m proud of the rolling, sandy seabed. Her size and length of 280ft makes this unlikely to be the *Angelus*, which was a 304 ton World War One trawler, but the size seems much too small for the *Maloja*, which was a 550ft long liner. However, there is a small wreck some 120yds to the south-west which is only 72ft long and could be the *Angelus*.

138 Grantham. British East Indiaman, built in 1742, sunk in 1744 when she hit the reef of Mole Rocks. Timbers have been found on the reef and artifacts revealed by side scan sonar at 51 04 44; 01 11 52E. A picture in the National Maritime Museum by Charles Brooking shows her in a storm with Sandgate Castle in the background. She is likely to become a protected wreck very soon; the Archaeological Diving Unit has visited the site. A team from Folkestone BSAC are working the site and say there are signs of at least four other wrecks on Mole Rocks.

139 Angelus. This is more likely the last resting place of this 304 ton Admiralty trawler than Site 137. The *Angelus* was mined and sank on February 28, 1916, at 51 04 44; 01 18 48E off Dover while on "Admiralty service". Depth is 27m and she lies north-south and stands 4m up from the seabed.

140 Lighter No.83. Lost in April 1944, this lighter lies north-south in very shallow water at 51 04 47; 01 12 38E. Depth is 9m and the sides of the lighter reach to within 3m of the surface. Only dive if there is nowhere else to go. It is near a sewer!

141 Maloja. One of the biggest wrecks in Kent waters and a victim of Oberleutnant Count von Schmettow in *UC-6* and the 12 mines he laid in a long diagonal line from north-west to south-east, 2 miles off Dover on the night of February 26-27, 1916.

Maloja was built in 1911 by Harland and Wolff for P & O and their London to Australia run. The 12,431 ton liner was 550ft long with a beam of 63ft and drew 34.

Sunk by mine in February 1916, the Maloja is one of the biggest wrecks in Kent waters.

Her quadruple expansion engines could push her along at a top speed of 19 knots. She was the largest vessel in the Company fleet at that time. On February 9, 1912, she was put on the Australia run via Colombo, Ceylon. On Saturday, February 26, 1916, she left Tilbury with 121 passengers and the same number of crew, for Bombay. Her captain, Commodore C.E. Irving, RNR, must have found her almost empty for she was designed to take 670 passengers. At 10.30am on Sunday, when she was some 2 miles south-west of Dover, there was a terrific explosion which blew in the side of the second saloon on the starboard side aft. The liner started to sink almost at once. Commodore Irving ordered the engines stopped and then reversed, to take the way off her and to allow the boats to be launched. But the engines, once reversed, could not be stopped and she was still going astern 29 minutes later when she sank with her props still spinning. As she went down she was listing so badly that she looked as though she was turning turtle. However, at that moment her boilers exploded. This seemed to right her and she went down upright.

As only a few boats were lowered, most survivors were the result of the large number of rafts she carried. In the end 122 passengers and crew, most of them engine room lascars, died. In many ways this was a repeat of the *Anglia* tragedy (see Site 122), even to the extent of another ship rushing to the rescue and hitting the same minefield. In this case it was the Canadian steamer *Empress of Fort William* (see Site 144) which sank in the rescue attempt.

Today the *Maloja* is largely covered with sand, though parts do stand up 5m at 51 04 51; 01 18 18E in a general depth of 21m. Salvage was carried out in 1964 by Risdon Beazley and dispersal was completed at the end of that year. Divers report this as an area of sand waves and so the wreck varies from year to year and almost from dive to dive. Her bow is to the south-west.

142 Corhaven. This collier of 991 tons was another victim of "Black Thursday" – July 25, 1940 – when the German Air Force tried to close the Channel to British shipping. The *Corhaven* was with Convoy CW8 and she was carrying 1244 tons of coal from the Tyne for Portsmouth when she was dive-bombed and sunk off Dover, though all 15 of her crew were saved. Today she lies on her starboard side with her bows to the north and across the tide at 51 04 91; 01 21 11E. She has been dived by Canterbury BSAC who found her in 32m, standing 5m proud. They describe her as mainly intact with anchor chains and cranes showing at the bow and the iron propeller and rudder in place at her stern. The cargo holds are open and easily accessible, though the Canterbury divers advise caution as the wreck is silty and easily stirred up. They add that the vis in the area is usually poor due to the nearby spoil ground where the dredgers from Dover Harbour dump their loads and as the cargo holds are so easily entered, in poor vis it would be quite easy for divers to find themselves inside the wreck without having intended to enter it.

143 The Tyre wreck. At 51 04 58; 01 17 13E. Named for her cargo of cement and tyres, this very old 250ft steamer is 4m proud in 20m and sitting on top of a mound on the seabed. She is very broken up. Name unknown.

144 Empress of Fort William. This was a Canadian steamer of 2181 tons, 250ft long with a beam of 43ft and a draught of 22. Commanded by Captain W.D. Shepherd, she steamed to the rescue of the *Maloja* (see Site 141) and ran into the same minefield which had claimed that liner as her first victim. The Canadian ship, built at Newcastle in 1908 as *Mount Stephen*, was owned at the time of her loss by the Express Transportation Co. of Midland and was carrying 3500 tons of coal from South Shields to Dunkirk. Hearing the first mine explode and seeing the liner well down by the stern, Captain Shepherd ordered full speed and told his crew to get the boats ready to help. Half an hour later he and his crew of 20 sat in those same boats and watched their own ship go down. Now she is at 51 05 00; 01 17 45E, hull intact, swept but upright, 7m proud, bow to the north in 24m.

145 Polgrange. A British collier of 804 tons, she was part of Convoy CW8 when she was sunk on "Black Thursday", July 25, 1940, by German dive bombers stationed on their newly captured airfields of Northern France (see Sites 42, 70, 135 and 142). The *Polgrange*, carrying 990 tons of coal from Blyth to Portsmouth and Cowes, had been attacked earlier on July 9, at 51 46 00; 01 46 00E, by German aircraft and damaged, but this time she did not escape a direct hit which killed 2 of her crew of 14. Now at 51 05 05; 01 20 16E, she lies with her cargo around her at 30m and a scour taking the depth down another 1m. She has her bow to the west and this is her highest point at 9m.

AREA 3:

Dover, South Foreland and St. Margaret's

Admiralty chart No.1828   **Ordnance Survey map 179**

This area runs from 51 05 20 to 51 10 00 and covers Dover, Dover Harbour, South Foreland, St. Margaret's Bay and north to Hope Point.

Dover is, of course, dominated by the white cliffs. On the western side of the town is the biggest of them all – Shakespeare Cliff, 338ft high. Standing on the top it is difficult to visualise what the Dover Straits must have looked like in times long past. The geologists say that the Straits were dry land, but low-lying. Then the floors of both the North Sea and the Channel rose and the sea flooded across. It is a good theory and would explain why the Straits are generally so shallow. The submarine ridges – the Ridens, Colbart and Varne – are high ground that stood up from the low flatlands before they were overwhelmed by the seas.

Dover has been England's main cross-Channel port for nearly 2000 years. This may seem like an exaggeration, but the Romans made it the base for their northern fleet and built a lighthouse in AD43, the remains of which can still be seen. Dover was a Cinque Port in the Middle Ages and its importance to British shipping is clearly shown by the massive castle built to guard it. The huge modern port covers a square mile and the outer harbour was completed in 1909 to shelter the great battleships of the Grand Fleet. Today cross-Channel ferries leave or arrive every few minutes and the Channel Tunnel is not expected to have much effect on that steady flow. During World War One, Dover was the centre of operations against the U-boats and the base for the ships of the Dover Patrol guarding the anti-submarine barrage of mines running right across the Channel from Folkestone to Cap Gris Nez. In World War Two Dover was shelled by German shore batteries and bombed by aircraft so often that it became known as Hellfire Corner.

High up at the Langdon Battery Centre near Swingate, overlooking Dover Harbour, is the headquarters of HM Coastguard which controls the traffic separation lanes in the Straits. It is also the centre for co-ordinating rescue operations from Beachy Head, Sussex, to Reculver Cliff near Herne Bay, Kent.

South Foreland is 1½ miles from the eastern entrance to Dover Harbour and

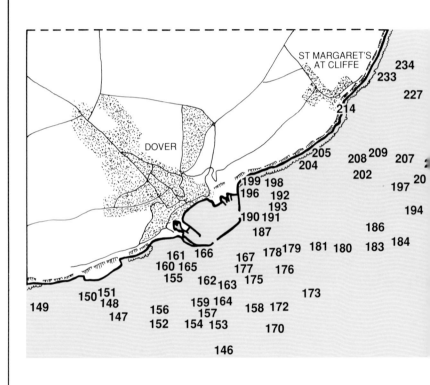

Dive Sites in Area 3

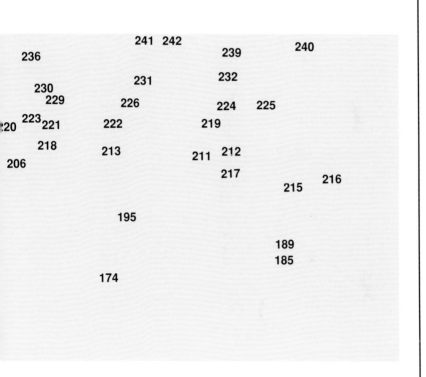

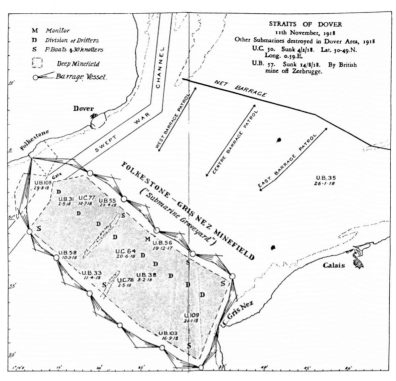

Above: S. Foreland lighthouse. Facing: Dover barrage, 1918; Dover Patrol Memorial.

from the sea stands out as a bold headland whose chalk cliffs have bands of flints in them. Two white lighthouses stand on the summit. The lower one (from which Marconi carried out early experiments) is disused and the other now operates automatically. It looks like a square castle tower and is 69ft high. A white windmill can be seen a quarter of a mile to the north-east of the lighthouse.

The chalk cliffs run right along the coastline of this area, but are broken at St. Margaret's at Cliffe, an easy run from Dover and much used by diving groups because of its easy launch. Channel swimmers often start from here. Those interested in diving U-boats will want to visit the Dover Patrol Memorial standing high on the cliffs just to the north of St. Margaret's. It is easily reached by car. The inscription reads: " To the Grace of God and in everlasting Memory of The Dover Patrol 1914-19." It was unveiled by the Prince of Wales on July 27th, 1921. There is also a later inscription which reads: "In Memory of the Officers and Men of the Royal Navy and Merchant Navy who gave their lives in ships sailing upon the Waters of the Dover Strait 1939-45." The tall stone memorial was erected with money given by the public. There is a similar memorial across the Channel at Cap Blanc Nez and another in New York Harbour. The names of casualties can be found in a book at the Dover Town Hall and another in the parish church at St. Margaret's at Cliffe.

Launching sites

Dover Harbour. This is a concrete slipway for use at all states of the tide. It is opposite the Royal Cinque Ports Yacht Club in Waterloo Crescent on the Marine Parade. Cars are not allowed on the promenade from which the slipway runs

down to the water. Trailers must be manhandled from the road over the prom. Speed limit in harbour: 8 knots.

St. Margaret's Bay. Turn off the A258 Dover-Deal road on B2058 for St. Margaret's at Cliffe, then continue down a steep winding road to the shore. Here there is a car park with a short wooden ramp over shingle at the northern end. At the other end is a pub called "The Coastguard" serving excellent pub grub. This pub, which also has a large car park, was rebuilt with beach flints after being hit by shellfire during World War Two. Various shelters and army defence works are carved out of the cliffs. But beware cliff falls – there was a very large one just to the east of the houses on the beach in March 1973. There is a toilet block at the back of the beach. The launching ramp is maintained by Dover District Council and their instructions for users of the ramp include not operating within 150m of the shore and going straight out for 150m before turning. Launching can be difficult in south winds.

Dover Harbour

Admiralty chart No. 1698   **Ordnance Survey map 179**

Channel 74 and 12   Dover Harbour Control: 0304 240400

Dover Harbourmaster is Captain P.R. White and he is responsible for all diving operations, including sport diving, in Dover Harbour. There is no diving in the

Looking north-east along Dover's Marine Parade to the port and castle.

harbour without his permission and it is very rarely given. Dive planners should note that the Harbourmaster's jurisdiction not only covers the harbour, but also the sea within a nautical mile of it and his permission is required here also.

All dive boats using Dover Harbour must carry VHF radio and use it. It is impossible to overstress the need for this and for the greatest care in boat handling near and in the harbour. Cross-Channel ferries, hovercraft, jetfoils and Sea Cats enter and leave the port by both east and west entrances every few minutes.

In fact Dover Port Control should be contacted by radio immediately before launching into the harbour, asking for permission to proceed. Port Control's instructions must be obeyed, as must any instructions from the Harbour Patrol Launch once afloat. Small craft, such as RIBs, must not be left unattended in the outer harbour, but buoys for short stays are available at £5 per day in the small craft anchorage near the shore end of the eastern side of Prince of Wales Pier and there are visitor berths (at 90p per metre per 24 hours) in the Wellington Dock Marina – tel: 0304 240400 – which is tidal. Gates open about 1½ hours before high water Dover to 1 hour after. Fuel is available in the Wellington Dock Marina and entry for this is free if the boat leaves on the same high water.

Port traffic signals are in operation day and night on panels near Port Control, eastern entrance and on Admiralty Pier at the western entrance. The signals are: DO NOT PROCEED – RED, RED, RED. PROCEED – GREEN, WHITE,GREEN. But specific permission to enter or leave must be obtained from Dover Port Control on VHF. While waiting for that permission, dive boats must stay well clear of the entrances.

Dover Port Control maintains a 24 hour listening watch on Channels 74, 12 or 16. Call sign: "Dover Port Control". Automatic radar VHF/DF indentification is in operation.

Dive boat cox'ns should also be aware that there are very strong tidal currents in and around both entrances, particularly in the period starting 2 hours before high water. And there can be strong tidal movements inside the harbour itself. It is not the lake it often looks.

Diving sites

146 Amplegarth. She was sunk at 51 05 20; 01 20 21E, in a field of six mines laid by Oberleutnant W. Marzecha in *UC-71* during the very early morning of April 10, 1918, off Dover. The *Amplegarth,* a British collier of 3707 tons, was 348ft long with a beam of 50ft and draught of 23 and was carrying 5820 tons of coal for the French Government from Dunstan-on-Tyne to St. Nazaire at the time of her loss. One of her crew was killed in the explosion. Now she lies in 32m and is upright and 11m proud.

147 Unknown, at 51 05 27; 01 16 31E. This 160ft long old steamer stands 5m proud of the seabed at 30m. No diving detail available.

148 Brandy Boat, or the Halcyon. At 51 05 36; 01 16 17E in 26m and charted as "foul". This wreck is very close to Site 150 and indeed it is difficult to sort out which ship is which. The discovery by local divers of a bell from the area inscribed *"Helene"* doesn't make things clearer. I would welcome help from any diver to sort things out. Until then I suggest you consult Site 150.

The beach at St. Margaret's at Cliffe, which boasts a short wooden slipway.

149 Empire Lough, a British steamer of 2824 tons, which was on her way from London to Gold Beach, Normandy with 2800 tons of cans of petrol for the tanks of the British 7th Armoured Division and other War stores when she was shelled by the German long-range shore batteries in France. She was badly damaged and was beached at 51 05 38; 01 14 40E. Her cargo was salvaged and sent to France by other ships. Today all you will find of her is a tangled mess of wreckage in a mere 8m with some pieces standing up 1-2m.

150 Halcyon. Also called the *Orangeman*. Might be the *Helene*. Certainly the bell divers brought up from her bore the name "Helene", which makes life difficult because the Admiralty says that this wreck is "probably" the *Halcyon,* a 300ft long British steamer of 1319 tons, which sank on April 7, 1916 after hitting a mine about 3 miles south-west by south of Folkestone Pier when heading home to London from Bordeaux with general cargo. All aboard were saved. The *Orangeman* seems to come about because the oranges salvaged from the ship were sold to help the survivors.

Whatever her real name is today her position is 51 05 38; 01 16 01E. She is on her port side with her bow to the north-west and up on a bank, which makes a great cavern under her. In the past few years much of the hull has started to collapse, but she is still 7m proud in 21m with a 3m scour. Her propeller is iron and her masts lie out on the shingle from the wreck. There is 15ft of silt in her after hold, which has train bogie wheels in it. In the forward hold are the remains of packing cases and a large number of broken bottles. In the galley area is broken crockery with a Rotterdam stamp. Her superstructure is beside her on the seabed. Diving is best 20 minutes either side of slack. The Salvage Association has an interest in recoveries.

151 Very small Unknown. At 51 05 41; 01 16 15E. Probably more Invasion debris, charted as "foul" in 20m.

152 Traquair. A small British collier of 1067 tons, 230ft long with a beam of 34ft and a draught of 15, she was lucky to escape from a U-boat in July 1915, but her luck ran out on January 12, 1916 when she hit a mine while on her way from Leith to Dunkirk with coal and general items. All her crew were saved. Now she is at 51 05 42; 01 18 53E, upright on the seabed and 8m proud in 26m. She has been swept.

153 Efford, part of. The *Efford* was cut in half in a collision on May 22, 1940. She was a small steamer of 339 tons and was in ballast at the time. This part of her stands 5m proud at 51 05 42; 01 20 14E in 25m. (See Site 157.)

154 Unknown. Not known to have been dived, but probably a steamer at 51 05 48; 01 19 37E. Stands 4m in 23m.

155 HMS Torbay II. This 82ft long requisitioned steam drifter was sunk at 51 05 49; 01 17 52E by bombs from a German aircraft on November 1, 1940, but no lives were lost. Today she stands 4m proud of a muddy seabed at 25m.

156 Unknown. At 51 05 54; 01 18 52E. Not identified, but thought to be a cargo steamer standing 4m proud in 22m on a very bumpy bottom.

157 Efford, part of. At 51 05 54; 01 19 43E. The other half of this small cargo steamer cut in two by a collision while she was travelling in ballast from the Tyne to Fowey on May 22, 1940. This section lies east-west and has a scour which takes the depth to 24m. She stands 6m proud and over 100ft long and is very broken up. (See Site 153.)

158 The Groove. At 51 05 56; 01 20 52E. Included as a curiosity. Found by the Admiralty on sonar, the "groove" or fissure in the seabed at 21m runs up and down Channel and is a little over 425ft in length.

159 Area of unknown wreckage. At 51 05 58; 01 19 38E. Charted as "foul", this is a big area of wreckage in 21m. Might be fishermen's dumping ground.

160 "Foul" area. At 51 06 27; 01 19 00E. Low wreckage less than 1m proud in 17m.

161 Unknown. At 51 06 33; 01 19 14E. Well sunk in and showing less than 1m in 12m. More likely to be rubbish than a shipwreck.

162 Another "foul" area. At 51 06 18; 01 20 09E. Wreckage here stands 1m proud in 15m.

163 "Foul" area. At 51 06 22; 01 20 18E. Wreckage 2m proud in 14m.

164 "Foul" area. At 51 06 34; 01 19 03E. Wreckage 2m high in 12m.

165 Unknown. Low wreckage only in 13m at 51 06 35; 01 20 19E. Charted as "foul".

166 HMS War Sepoy. Very little remains of this World War One Z-type standard tanker at 51 06 42; 01 19 45E and what does is really undiveable, lying as she does so close to Dover Harbour's western entrance. Her position is not surprising, as she was sunk in the entrance during World War Two as a blockship.
War Sepoy was built by William Gray and Co. of West Hartlepool under the Standardised Shipbuilding Scheme to replace the vast losses caused by the German U-boat campaign. She was 412ft long with a beam of 52ft, could travel at 11 knots with a full cargo of oil and was of 5800 tons gross. But she was launched too late for the War on December 5, 1918, and was not completed until February 6, 1919. In 1921 she was handed over to the Admiralty as a fleet oiler. On July 19, 1940, she was damaged and burnt out in a German air raid on Dover Harbour. Beyond repair, she was filled with concrete, towed into position and sunk as a blockship at the western entrance to the harbour. They started to remove her in 1950 and found her fore part was lying alongside the World War One blockship *Spanish Prince.* (See Site 167). The bridge of the *War Sepoy* collapsed forward over that old wreckage when her stern was removed to open the entrance on April 26, 1964. Diving without permission of the Dover Harbourmaster is forbidden.

167 Spanish Prince. At 51 06 47; 01 19 51E. This was a World War One blockship. She is now totally broken and is charted as a "foul" anchorage after removal operations started in 1931. Dover Harbour Board surveyed her wreckage in 1990

The W.A. Scholten: lost after a collision in November 1887. (See site 168.)

and found the highest point to be 1.1m in 11m. No diving without permission of the Dover Harbourmaster.

168 W.A. Scholten. The remains of this 2589 ton early Dutch liner lie at 51 04 54; 01 24 40E after a collision in November, 1887. Her captain, G.H. Taat, his first officer, and 130 passengers and crew were drowned. They had been bound from Rotterdam for New York. The liner, built in 1874 on the Clyde by Robert Napier and Sons for the Nederlandsch-Amerikaansche Stoomv. Maats, was 351ft long with a beam of 38 and a draught of 19. Her compound inverted engines of 360hp could push her along at 10 knots. She was not going quite as fast as that on the evening of November 19, 1887, when she was about 4 miles east of Dover, as there was a thick haze – almost a fog – over the sea.

The captain of another ship, the collier *Rosa Mary* of West Hartlepool, thought

Plates recovered from the wreck of the early Dutch liner W.A. Scholten.

73

it too thick to go on, so at 10.20pm he anchored and hoped that the mist would lift. Suddenly the lights of the *Scholten* loomed out of the murk and the liner crashed into his starboard bow. The impact was tremendous and the *Rosa Mary* was badly damaged but managed to stay afloat and at daybreak struggled into Dover Harbour where Captain Webster said that he was at anchor when the liner ran into him. The surviving officers of the *Scholten* told a different story. They said they too had anchored, but when the fog began to lift got under way again. They saw the lights of the *Rosa Mary* indicating she was at anchor, but when they came closer they found she was steaming right at them and she crashed into them.

Though the *Scholten* was much bigger, she suffered more damage. There was an 8ft wide hole in her port bow and the water pouring in gave her a heavy list to port. There were 156 passengers aboard and a crew of 54. The list to port made it impossible to launch lifeboats to carry all of them. Two did get away and many passengers, in lifebelts, were rescued from the sea by lines thrown from the Sunderland steamer *Ebro*, which arrived on the scene together with a fishing boat. Twenty minutes after the collision the *Scholten* went down by the head. At that moment the haze lifted, but only 78 of those aboard the liner were saved.

Today the *Scholten* is 12m proud at her highest points – the collapsed wheel-house, boilers and engine room. Most of her hull is intact and upright, though there are clear signs of damage to her bow, near the site of her foremast. There is no superstructure left and her decking is collapsing inwards. Depth to the seabed is 33m. Her bows face to the north-east and there is a deep scour.

Some of the best recoveries from the wreck have been fine plates and bowls decorated with coloured pastoral scenes. Marks on the back identify them as made in Maastricht, in south-east Holland. However, it was a piece of a large serving plate from the crew area which clinched her identity – it bore the marks "NASM" and "Rotterdam" on it. Divers who miss landing exactly on her might find a bonus. Her massive telegraph, which needed two big lifting bags to get it to the surface, slipped from the lashings, plunging to the seabed close to the wreck and couldn't be relocated.

169 HMS Peridot. An Admiralty trawler of 398 tons completed in 1933, which was mined off Dover on March 15, 1940, she is at 51 05 36; 01 25 44E.She stands 10m proud in 30m and is all in one piece despite sweeping. Highest point is her bow, which points to the north-east. Her gun is level and points aft.

170 Unknown. At 51 05 35; 01 21 21E. A steamer 10m proud in 30m, lying almost exactly east-west and about 310ft long. Has been swept, but a good part of her superstructure has survived.

171 Unknown. Looks like a World War Two cargo ship with a single cast-iron pro-peller still in place.This is easy to see, because she is completely upside down with her keel about 7m proud of the seabed of sand and fine shale at 30m at 51 03 45; 01 22 03E. The hull has numerous holes at various places along its length. At bow and stern it is possible to swim under the wreck. She lies across the tide with her bows to the south-south-east.

172 MTB. This site at 51 05 55; 01 21 18E has not yet been dived but is showing a clear outline on sonar of a motor torpedo boat or similar coastal forces vessel, lying north-east to south-west, and a slim 89ft long, standing 4m in 25m.

173 Unknown steamer. At 51 06 07; 01 22 06E and about 256ft long in 29m and standing nearly 10m proud.

174 U-11. One of the first U-boats to use the newly captured port of Zeebrugge in November 1914. Though the Flanders Flotilla didn't officially come into being until March 29, 1915, this one was believed by both the Germans and the British to have been lost in a British minefield outside Zeebrugge. Commanded by Kapitanleutnant Fritz von Suchodoletz, *U-11* was 188ft long, could do 14 knots on the surface and 8 submerged and was paraffin fueled. She had two bow and two stern tubes and carried six 45cm torpedoes for them. She failed to make radio contact on December 9, 1914, so that is presumed to be the date of her sinking. There were no survivors. How she came to be in her present position – 51 06 20; 01 29 45E – no one knows. She is intact in 46m and stands 9m proud of the shingle bed.

175 Unknown. A steamer about 180ft long, standing 4m proud in 19m at 51 06 27; 01 21 04E, there is a 2m scour around her. She is well broken. More diving details required.

176 Unknown, at 51 06 28; 01 21 30E, is a steamer about 150ft long standing 5m proud in 21m and lying with her bows to the south-west.

177 Lady Stella. At 51 06 34; 01 20 54E. This British motor vessel of 5160 tons sank after a collision with the Royal Mail steamer *Pardo* on June 7, 1958. Since then she has been heavily dispersed after chain sweeping, so much so that her wreckage is well spread over the seabed and is only 2m high in a general depth of 18m.

178 Unknown. At 51 06 42; 01 21 30E. More diving detail needed – at the moment this is just a wreck found on sonar, 16m to the top of her, 21m to the seabed.

179 Unknown. A 240ft long steamer, standing 5m proud in 20m at 51 06 44; 01 21 42E. Salvage was carried out in 1964, but no details available.

180 Unknown. At 51 06 45; 01 22 57E. A small steamer just 100ft long, lying north-east to south-west in a depth of 27m and standing 4m proud of the seabed.

181 Unknown. At 51 06 45; 01 22 34E. Another small one, 78ft long in 24m and standing 3m proud.

182 Unknown, but mainly intact, old steamer lying with her bows to the north. She is completely over on her starboard side with her rudder in place, but her propeller has been salvaged or is certainly missing. The highest point on her side is 6m above the sand at 30m. Appears to be of at least World War One vintage. At 51 04 20; 01 22 54E.

183 Unknown. At 51 06 46; 01 23 57E. Lying with bow to south-east in 26m and 6m proud at the highest part, this wreck is of a ship about 150ft long.

184 Unknown. Almost completely buried in sand-mud at 51 06 48; 01 24 27E, this wreck has a little scour around her and at the highest shows only 3m above the seabed at 26m.

185 MTB 218. This British motor torpedo boat of 35 tons, completed and handed over for service on June 9, 1941, was lost on August 18, 1942 after being crippled by a German E-boat and then limping on to a mine. The 65ft MTB now lies on seabed of sand and broken shells at 51 06 52; 01 37 10E. She is upright and intact and lies exactly north-south in 39m, from which she stands 7m proud.

186 HMS Rodino. An old British Admiralty trawler of 230 tons, dating back to 1913, she was one of the Navy ships trying to see that the convoys could get through the Channel in July, 1940. But the German dive bombers got her on July 24 and today she is at 51 07 00; 01 23 55E, with her 100ft hull north-west to south-east on the seabed at 27m. She is badly damaged from the bomb which sank her, but stands 5m proud. Sunk same day as *Kingston Galena* (see Site 194).

187 Wreckage. At 51 07 01;01 20 59E. Charted as "foul", this wreckage stands less than 1m high in 15m.

188 Unknown. A big steamer with a 33ft beam, this one is at 51 07 03; 01 25 53E, has her bows to the south-east in 25m and stands 3m proud. She has been swept. Local divers have recovered a brass plate bearing the word "Brussels" and her bridge telegraph, but there is no further clue so far to her identity.

189 Unknown. About 130ft long, this wreck at 51 07 07; 01 35 28E has had her superstructure ripped off, presumably by sweeping, and though well buried in her own scour at 44m must be an iron ship or was carrying a cargo of ammunition, judging by the magnetometer of one dive boat!

190 Fancy. A 26ft long British gaff cutter, which sank on January 28, 1974. Today she is smashed to pieces at 51 07 12; 01 20 51E some 300yds east of Dover Harbour entrance. No diving without permission of the Harbourmaster and probably not worth it anyway.

191 Wreckage. Charted as "foul" at 51 07 13; 01 21 12E, this wreckage stands less than 1m in 13m.

192 Wreckage. Another small area of low wreckage, less than 1m high at 51 07 15; 01 21 12E and charted as foul.

193 Barge. At 51 07 18; 01 20 44E. Intact and believed to have sunk over 20 years ago. In 11m and 3m proud.

194 HMS Kingston Galena. A 550 ton Admiralty trawler completed in 1934 and sunk by dive bombers of the same Luftwaffe squadron which sank the *Rodino*, another Navy trawler, earlier the same day, July 24, 1940. Today she lies at 51 07 18; 01 24 52E in 25m from which she is 5m proud. She is in three parts. One is completely upright and includes the bow. Another lies almost upside down. The third lies on the port side and is the stern. There are depth-charges on it. *Warning* – Divers from London who drifted just 200yds south of the main wreckage found three 8-10ft long cylinders, 3.5ft in diameter, badly corroded with three lifting points on each at their vented ends. The divers thought they looked like "block-buster bombs"!

195 UC-46. Commanded by Oberleutnant Franz Moecke, *UC-46* sank five ships with mines and torpedoes in 1916 and another five in the early days of 1917, making his final total ten ships – 10,660 tons in all. Moecke's last mission started from Zeebrugge on January 25, 1917. He went through the Dover barrage without incident, laid his mines in the Bristol Channel and on the way back and near Breaksea Point saw the 275 ton Admiralty trawler *Longset* sink on one of them. After sinking a further three vessels and badly damaging another, he headed home on the night of February 7-8 and ran safely through the Dover Barrage submerged. Unfortunately for Moecke, he surfaced at 3.09am in bright moonlight right in the path of the Navy destroyer *Liberty*, which promptly fired a shot at the U-boat while heading for her at 24 knots. Lt-Commander P.W.S. King, RN, saw the shot go wide and decided to ram the submarine. Moecke may just have had time to see the destroyer bearing down on him through his periscope, but he had no time to do anything else. The *Liberty* hit *UC-46* at full speed, just 2ft in front of the conning tower, and rammed her bow 4ft deep into the submarine. The U-boat sank at once, but Commander King was not satisfied and rained depth charges into the bubbles of air and oil on the surface. There were no survivors from the U-boat crew of 26. Commander King was awarded the D.S.O.

Today *UC-46* is on the bottom at 51 07 13; 01 30 07E in 35m, 161ft long with a beam of 17, her 8.8cm gun still on the deck in front of the conning tower and just ahead of the point where the *Liberty* rammed her. Her mine shafts, which carried 18 mines, are empty, and further towards the bow. Her bow is to the north-west, down a slope in the rocky seabed.

196 Bronze Age arms trader. This is the scene of one of Britain's oldest shipwrecks and was discovered by Simon Stevens, Mike Hadlow and Alan Moat of Dover BSAC on a dive in Langdon Bay, just east of Dover Harbour on August 14, 1974. In the gullies in the bay are relics of various wars from cannon balls to World War Two shells. At first the Dover divers thought they had discovered wedges which were once used to hold railway lines to sleepers, but because they looked very old took them to Dover Museum which quickly identified them as Bronze Age winged daggers and spearheads. Since then hundreds of similar bronze weapons have been recovered and are now in the possession of the British Museum, which bought them from Dover BSAC so that the hoard could be kept together. The site was designated a protected wreck site (under the Protection of Wrecks Act of 1973) in 1978 with Alan Moat as the licensee and Martin Dean as archaeological director.

In 1978 the order forbade diving within 75m of 51 07 36; 01 20 48E and in 1979 that area was increased to a radius of 150m of that position. The finds are believed to have been the cargo of a Bronze Age arms trader and come from central Europe dating from about 1100 BC.

197 HMS Bonar Law. This Admiralty-hired trawler of 284 tons sank on October 27, 1915, after a collision off the South Goodwins. She is now broken but 5m proud in 27m with a scour around her in a north-south position at 51 07 38; 01 24 39E.

198 Sigrid. This Dutch three-masted schooner of 100 tons is now at 51 07 40; 01 21 02E, but this is not where the 88ft long ship first sank on November 9, 1975. Then she capsized after engine failure and while under tow of the m.v. *Tove Lonborg* within a few yards of the entrance to Dover Harbour. She was a hazard to navigation and was lifted and moved out of the way to her present position on November 24. Bits of her are now to be found sticking out of the seabed at 5m.

199 Summity. Awash at low water at 51 07 42; 01 20 52E. This 554 ton motor vessel was one of Convoy CW8 on "Black Thursday" – July 25, 1940 – and coming down Channel when the German Air Force attacked from their new bases in Occupied France (see Site 135). The *Summity*, which was carrying a cargo of cement, was hit in the cement-filled holds once and suffered further damage from three near-misses by Stuka dive bombers off Dover. Covered in cement dust, and sinking, she was beached by her captain. Her steel mast and some plating have occasionally been used in recent years as an exercise mark by Air-Sea Rescue helicopters.

200 Falcon. This 675 ton steamer was outward bound from Belgium when she caught fire on October 26, 1926. She was taken in tow, but so big was the fire that the towline burnt through. She drifted ashore at Langdon Steps the next day at 51 07 52; 01 21 07E, where only bottom plates remain.

201 Toward. A British merchant steamer of 1218 tons carrying a general cargo from London to Belfast, she sank after hitting a mine on October 31, 1915. All aboard were saved. The mine was one of four laid parallel to the shore "off the Southern entrance to the Downs" by Oberleutnant Count von Schmettow in

Above: the merchant steamer Toward. Opposite: the Preussen aground in Crab Bay.

UC-6 during the night of October 30-31. *Toward,* built in 1899 and owned by the Clyde Shipping Co. of Glasgow, was 250ft long with a beam of 35 and draught of 16, and was one of 54 ships sunk by the actions of *UC-6* during the war.

Now she is at 51 07 44; 01 25 02E, lies east to west and has her bow separated from the rest of her. She seems to have split apart just in front of the bridge. Her bow is 30ft away from her body and is standing upright with the bow-tip pointing to the surface. She has been wire-swept. She is 8m proud in 25m. Tony Goodfellow of Gillingham, Kent, who owns her together with Sid Meadows and Dave Knight, says they do not mind anyone diving her, but object strongly to anyone taking anything from the wreck. He warns that the debris in the break where the bow snapped off is unstable and dangerous to divers.

202 Emma. This 990 ton Swedish steamer of 233ft with a beam of 28ft and a draught of 16 sank at 51 07 56; 01 23 47E following a collision with a French ship on June 3, 1940. Now she lies with her bow to the north, 7m proud in 25m. She has been swept and is broken in half. Divers have recovered a number of porcelain figures from her. They are of animals and people on a bridge and were coloured, but are now mostly white as a result of the sea stripping off the paint. There are also metal ingots on board. These are stamped "Babbetts Patent Crown".

203 Eidsiva. A Norwegian steamer of 1092 tons, 229ft long with a beam of 35ft and a draught of 16. She was carrying coal to France when she hit a mine on October 31, 1915 – one in the same minefield laid by Oberleutnant Count von Schmettow in *UC-6* which sank the *Toward* on the same day (see Site 201). Today she is at 51 07 59; 01 25 15E, lying on her port side and 10m proud in 27m. Her cargo of coal is scattered around her. All her crew were saved.

204 Preussen. The largest steel sailing ship of her time, 5081 tons and 5 masts, 408ft long with a beam of 53ft and a draught of 27, she was carrying a general cargo, including cement and 100 pianos, from Hamburg to Valparaiso when she was in collision with the cross-Channel steamer *Brighton*. The sailing ship was badly damaged and started taking in water. Tugs tried to get Captain Nissen and his ship into Dover, but towlines snapped in the gale and *Preussen* drove ashore in Crab Bay on November 6, 1910, at 51 08 01; 01 22 10E. The German crew stayed aboard and the Kaiser sent a telegram of encouragement, but she was too badly stove in by the rocks under her to be moved. Today her wreckage is still there, broadside to the great chalk cliffs. Steel plates litter the bottom amid the weeds, and the outlines of the barrels of cement run the length of one forehold; most of the pianos were salvaged. The wreck is easy to find – some of her ribs still stick up above the surface at low water.

205 Notre Dame de Lourdes. This 47 ton French vessel was fishing in the Channel when stopped and boarded by a U-boat. The boarding party planted charges to sink her, but although they went off, the ship drifted without sinking until she finally stranded at 51 08 01; 01 22 10E on March 1, 1917. Very little of her remains today.

206 The Queen. There are two version about how this 1676 ton wartime transport, which had been the first cross-Channel turbine ship ever built, was actually sunk on October 26, 1916. There is no dispute, however, that what caused it was a raid by German destroyers, mostly reinforcements newly arrived in the captured Belgian ports, on the ships of the Dover Patrol. Nor is there any argument about the fact that she was abandoned by all her crew when surprised and fired upon by those same destroyers, thereby giving the Germans an easy capture. *The Queen* (not just "Queen", but *The* Queen) was travelling empty, except for a few bags of mail – troops were not carried at night – when returning from Boulogne to Folkestone. At about 11pm she was stopped "3 miles north-east of the Varne Light Vessel", but Admiralty records are not clear about exactly how the Germans disposed of their prize. One version says a German boarding party planted bombs and opened her sea-cocks, the other states that she was torpedoed by one of the German destroyers. Either way, it took her some time to sink and she was carried by the tidal stream to her present position of 51 08 03; 01 27 24E.

The Queen was far from being the only casualty of that moonless October

Above left: engine-room telegraph from the WWI transport ship The Queen (pictured).

The WWI armed trawler Othello II: a minefield victim now lying in 27m.

night. The 28 drifters which were watching over the barrage of wire-nets with mines attached across the Straits were badly hit by the destroyers – 7 drifters were sunk and 3 severely damaged, with 45 men killed and 10 taken prisoner.

One old 30-knotter British destroyer, HMS *Flirt,* mistook the Germans for British destroyers, even though when she challenged them they gave her the wrong light signal in reply. She learned her mistake when she later lowered a boat to pick up the swimming crew of a Dover Patrol drifter. Suddenly the 215ft long war-ship was lit up by searchlights on the German destroyers and she was sunk so quickly that the only survivors were the men in her rescue boat. Divers have not yet found her wreck.

Later that night another destroyer, HMS *Nubian,* also mistook the Germans for friends. She was torpedoed and had her bows blown off, though she did not sink, but drifted ashore. Her stern was later combined with the bows of another destroyer, HMS *Zulu,* which had been mined, to make the destroyer *Zubian* (see Site 3).

Today *The Queen* sits upright 8m proud of the seabed at 27m, with her bows to the north-west. She is silting badly on her starboard side and is collapsing inwards, with her stern sunk in deeper than her bow. The wreck was positively identified by portholes bearing the builder's name and the recent discovery of a small named bell.

207 HMS Othello II. This 206 ton armed Admiralty trawler was No.1193 and part of the Dover minesweeping force when she became yet another victim of *UC-6's* October 30 minefield. On October 31, 1915, she was ordered by Commander W.G. Rigg, the Minesweeping Officer, Dover, to move to "Section Two" which was the code for the area between the Goodwin Gate and the Gull Light Ship. It was as she battled to get there against a strong gale from the south-south-east that she hit a mine at 11.55am. The explosion broke her nearly in two and she started sinking immediately. The wheelhouse was so distorted by the explosion that neither the door nor the windows would open.

Trapped inside as the water rose up around them were the skipper, the second-in-command (the "second hand"), the helmsman and a deck boy. The three men managed to squeeze the boy out of a partly open window, but could not follow themselves. The boy was the only one saved out of the ten aboard. (See Site 220.) As a result of this incident, orders were given to remove all the sliding doors of the trawlers' wheelhouses and to replace them with canvas screens which could be pushed out in an emergency. This is said to have saved a number of lives in later sinkings.

Today the *Othello II* lies at 51 08 04; 01 24 40E with her bows to the east in 27m, though a scour increases that to 29m. The wreck is about 100ft long and stands 5m proud. She has been positively identified by her builder's plate.

208 White Rose. This wooden sailing vessel has been dived but is very broken. It is doubtful if *White Rose* is really her name. Local divers laugh when asked about her, saying that the only reason she is called that is because pottery from her bore the initials "W.R". Her bows, her highest point at 3m, lie to the north-east and she is in 25m at 51 08 05; 01 23 38E.

209 HMS Aries. Twenty-two hands were lost and nine saved when this Admiralty hired yacht of 268 tons, used for boarding and inspecting suspect vessels, was sunk by a mine "off Leathercoat" on October 31, 1915, on the same day and in the same minefield as *Othello II* (see Site 207), the *Toward* (see Site 201) and the *Eidsiva* (see Site 203). Today the 197ft former pleasure craft with a 50ft beam is broken with her bow to the south-east, but is more or less complete at 51 08 07; 01 23 48E. She has been identified by her crockery.

210 Hundvaag, but may be only her stern. At 51 08 08; 01 26 46E. Local divers say this is a steamer's stern lying east-west, about 190ft long with a beam of 50, upright but silting heavily on both sides, and 6m proud in 28m. Identified by Scandinavian pottery, but Admiralty place the *Hundvaag* much further to the north-east. (See Site 223.)

211 Unknown. At 51 08 08; 01 32 00E. A wreck almost completely silted over and about 450ft long in 46m.

212 Saint Ronan. A 568 ton British trawler sunk on July 11, 1959, at 51 08 10; 01 32 40E in 50m general depth, but one in which great rolling sandbanks suggest that the trawler is upright on top of one of them, which makes the depth to her highest point only 36m.

213 Francesco Ciampa. This 3611 ton Italian steamer was sunk on February 11, 1927, following a collision near the South Goodwin Light Vessel while on her way from Benisaf to Rotterdam with a cargo of iron ore. This ship was built in Britain in 1899 by T. Turnbull and Son with 282hp triple expansion engines. She was 352ft long with a beam of 43ft and a draught of 21 and was owned by F.S. Ciampa and Figli, which might account for her name! Today her hull is split in two and the stern section has a 3m scour around and under it. Divers say that sweeping has totally removed her superstructure, but she is mostly upright at 51 08 13; 01 29 44E. Depth is 27m and her highest point is her bow, 9m proud. A bank of sand hangs over her on the north side.

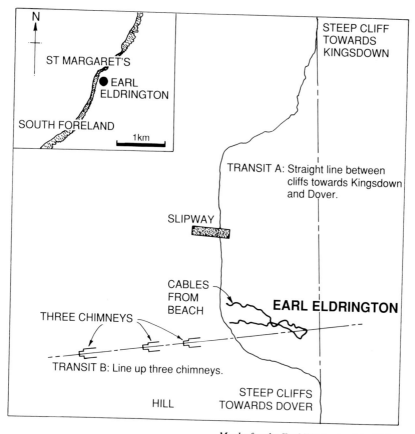

Marks for the Earl Eldrington (site 214).

214 Earl Eldrington. Ran ashore in St. Margaret's Bay. Stands 1m proud in 10m on sand seabed. A dive for beginners, with keel and keelson standing out of the bottom with big brass rivets sticking out. About 30m of keel exposed, hull collapsed into sand, but exposed timber in good condition. Cables on the beach lead to within 2yds of the wreck. Some of her timbers were used to build a beach hut, but this was destroyed during World War Two.

215 German Destroyer G-42, or possibly *G-85.* Both torpedoboat-destroyers failed to return from a five warship raid on the drifters watching over the anti-U-boat nets stretching from the Goodwins to Snouw Bank. Unfortunately for the Germans they ran into two British destroyers, *Swift* and *Broke,* in the darkness. *Broke,* commanded by Commander Edward R.G.R. Evans, torpedoed the second ship in the German line, rammed the third and fought a battle with bayonets and cutlasses with the Germans who boarded as the two ships were locked together. When the ships broke free Evans torpedoed another German ship before switching on his searchlights and picking up the survivors from the ship he had rammed and which had now sunk. One of the victims of "Evans of the Broke" – as he was always called after that engagement of April 21, 1917 – lies at 51 08 17; 01 34 57E. Both were built in Krupp's Germania yard (hence the code letter "G") and were of 1147 tons, 273ft long with a beam of 27ft, and could do 34 knots. Their armament was three 4.1in guns, two machine guns and six torpedo tubes mounted on the deck. The depth is 48m, from which the destroyer is over 10m proud.

216 Carmen. This Panamanian steamer of 4240 tons was involved in an amazing quadruple series of collisions. She was on her way from Takoradi to Burntisland with a cargo of bauxite on June 13, 1963. The 370ft long ship with a beam of 53ft and a draught of 23 was feeling her way up Channel in the early morning in thick fog when she was hit by the Turkish steamer *Sadikzade.* Her master and 20 crew took to the boats before she sank, though two men were lost. *Sadikzade* then collided with the Greek m.v *Leandros,* which in turn collided with the British motor tanker *Clyde Sergeant.* All three of the other ships made port. But *Carmen,* built in 1930, now lies at 51 08 17; 01 36 26E in 43m. She is 17m proud but this is a mast, as she is upright with all her superstructure intact. She was to be swept recently.

217 Andaman. A Swedish 4765 ton motorship of Gothenburg, 439ft long with a beam of 59ft and draught of 21, built in 1947 by A/B Gotaverken, she was in collision on May 24, 1953, near the South Goodwins Light Ship with the Panamanian ship *Fortune.* In thick fog, the *Andaman* started sinking at once and her crew of 38 took to the boats. They were picked up by the steamer *Arthur Wright* and later transferred to the Dover lifeboat.

Some salvage, particularly her 10 ton phosphor-bronze propeller, has been carried out on the wreck at 51 08 21; 01 33 57E. She is still mainly intact and lies with her bow to the south-east – she was bound for Calcutta from Gothenburg – and stands a massive 24m from the seabed at 49m. Her height and position in a strong tidal stream means that there is often a great tide rip over her. *Treasure Footnote–* The *Andaman* was carrying bullion. Part of her cargo consisted of eight ingots of silver, each weighing no less than 30lb. One was brought ashore by one of the ship's officers. There is no report of the rest of the ingots being salvaged.

218 Mystery Submarine at 51 08 23; 01 28 20E. It seems likely that if this was a submarine (for missing ones see Site 73) then she has now dived under the sand of the seabed here at 20m and is charted as "foul". That there was a wreck is not open to doubt. She was first traced by the Navy in 1940 and gave the perfect echo for a bottomed submarine. Over the years one survey ship after another kept finding something and a drift sweep, though clear at 19.8m, was very definitely "foul" at 20.1m in 1969. In 1971 it was clear that the wreck, whatever it was, was sliding down a slope of sand. By 1981 she wasn't showing above the sand of the seabed and in 1991 there was no trace of her at all, but the sand is on the move and she may soon be exposed again.

219 HMS The Boys. At 51 08 30; 01 32 12E. This Admiralty drifter of 92 tons built in 1914 sank here in heavy weather on November 14, 1940. Depth is 46m. No further details available.

220 HMS Weigelia. This steel Admiralty trawler of 262 tons, 125ft long with a beam of 22 and draught of 12, was sunk by a mine on February 28, 1916, at 51 08

Bell from the wreck of the South Goodwins Light Vessel No. 69.

32; 01 27 13E. It is interesting to note that the boy survivor from the wheelhouse of the *Othello II* (see Site 207) was sent to join *Weigelia* after he had recovered, and was on board when she was sunk. He survived again and only one man was lost from her crew. Today the broken wreck of the *Weigelia* is on the seabed at 25m and stands 5m proud at her highest point, the bow.

221 South Goodwin Light Vessel No. 69. This 165ft long "floating lamp" was unmanned when she disappeared during the calm night of October 25-26, 1940. It was believed at the time that the Light Vessel went because of "enemy action", and it is true that Trinity House demanned all the light vessels because of the casualties on the East Coast when the Luftwaffe started using the light ships for target practice. At one time the Trinity House tenders were armed, but then this was stopped and great notices on the tenders' sides said "Lighthouse Service", but they were still attacked.

Today No. 69 is intact except for a big hole in her port bow, upright but becoming buried at 51 08 36; 01 28 13E. At present she is 3m proud in 25m. Her deck is mangled, which might suggest a bombing attack. Her bell, marked "LV 69", has been recovered.

222 Freshwater spring. No, not the name of a ship, but this may be the reason for strange soundings near a small wreck 3m proud in 27m at 51 08 37; 01 29 47E.

223 Hundvaag. A small Norwegian steamer of 690 tons used by the Navy as a collier, this 183ft ship with a beam of 29ft was mined on November 1, 1940 "approximately 1-2 cables west of No.1 Buoy, which was formerly the S. Goodwins LV". The ship was on its way from Immingham to Dover, carrying 760 tons of coal for the Admiralty, when she hit the mine which killed one of the crew. The other 14 and a pilot were saved. She lies north-south at 51 08 41; 01 27 55E in 25m on a flat seabed of hard sand and is in two parts about 200ft apart. Both are upright with 8m the highest point. A depth charge lies close to her on the sand. (See Site 210.)

224 Unknown. At 51 08 52; 01 32 28E. A steamer of abut 260ft with a beam of 49ft, she is sliding down the side of a steep slope and at present is some 6m proud in 34m, but the slope falls away steeply ahead of her!

225 Sambut. A Liberty ship and one of the "Sam" ships (see Site 34). Of 7176 tons, 423ft × 57ft × 35ft, she started life in the Oregon Building Corporation yard at Portland in August 1943 as the *C.M. Jones,* but was completed 17 days later (the yard was building 16 Liberty ships a month in 1943) as the *Sambut.* During the War she was managed by P.Henderson and Co. of Glasgow. On D-Day, June 6, 1944, the *Sambut,* commanded by Captain M. Willis, left the Southend anchorage at 6am and headed for the Invasion beaches, just one of the huge Eastern fleet heading for Normandy. She had nearly 1000 troops and 137 armoured vehicles aboard as well as ammunition and petrol in jerry cans stacked on the foredeck. She carried a crew of 40 and 23 gunners manning the AA guns. As she was passing Dover, two ships abreast, she was spotted by a German long-range shore battery near Calais. Two German shells struck her amidships at noon and she was soon ablaze, with ammunition exploding in all directions. One of the German shells burst in No. 4 mess-deck. It was packed with troops and 150 of them were killed. The port lifeboats were destroyed, but the starboard boats were safely launched. Still ablaze, the abandoned ship drifted to the Goodwins and sank.

Today she is at 51 08 52; 01 33 27E on a flat shingle seabed at 51m from which she stands 19m proud, intact and with her bows to the south-south-west. Her height makes finding her a matter of looking for the large swirls down tide. A local salvage company has asked for permission to sink an unwanted concrete caisson alongside the wreck.

226 Eleonora, formerly called the Obotrita. A West German m.v. of 499 tons coming from Cadiz to Felixstowe with a cargo of 66 containers of wine was in collision with the Belgian cross-Channel ferry *Prinses Maria Esmeralda* on May 30, 1979. In the collision her deck cargo — 18 containers of wine — broke free, but the damage to her below decks was much more severe and she sank at 51 08 55; 01 30 08E. Today the 254ft long ship with a beam of 43ft, lies in 26m and is 7m proud. Some salvage work has been carried out and she has been cleared to 18m. Her hull is still upright and there are still wine containers in the wreckage.

227 Loanda. An early steamer of 2702 tons, built in 1891, 328ft long with a beam of 39ft and a draught of 22. She was travelling from Hamburg to the west coast of Africa with a general cargo for the Elder Dempster Line when she collided with a Russian steamer called *Junona.* The *Loanda* came off worse, being hit on the port side near the engine room. Dover tugs pulled her towards the shore, but she finally sank stern first at 51 08 57; 01 24 43E on May 31, 1908. She now lies in 20m and is 7m proud, though the sand tends to crawl over her. She is upright, has been swept and dispersed. Her 253hp triple expansion steam engine,

The 2702-ton Loanda: sunk in 1908, and now one of the most popular Kent dives.

installed by her builders, the Naval Construction and Armaments Co., can now be clearly seen where her superstructure has been ripped off.

This is one of the most popular of all Kent dives, with divers finding such souvenirs as clay pipes and all kinds of bottles, including small scent bottles. Her forecastle bell was recovered two years ago. Salvage rights to her have been bought by amateur divers Paul Wilkinson, Peter Lee and Mick Lucas, who are recovering porcelain and other material from her cargo. They say sport divers are welcome to continue diving her, but would ask them now to confine their souvenirs to bottles from the numerous cases of gin aboard ("all the contents are undrinkable") as well as champagne bottles which also contain similar "vile stuff" now the sea has done its work. There have been rumours of thousands of newly minted silver shillings aboard, but there is certainly no sign of them on her cargo manifest, which lists such items as hundreds of cases of gin, rum and champagne – and a similar amount of gunpowder – nor have any of the hundreds who have dived her ever found a single coin. Of course there was a good deal of salvage at the time, but nothing in this line was ever declared.

228 HMS Unknown. An armed trawler at 51 09 06; 01 25 41E, 6m proud in 21m. The letters CYO, or GYO, 18 were found on part of the wreckage of her funnel by divers, who report that she has been swept as her superstructure lies out 30ft to port. Her bow is complete but she has been blown amidships. There are shell cases on the wreck.

229 HMS Cayton Wyke. A British anti-sub trawler of 373 tons, she was caught by a German E-boat on July 8, 1940, off Dover and torpedoed. First dived in 1984 by amateur divers, she was found to be intact, though the attack had caused considerable damage to her hull on the port side. Her wheelhouse and decking were then fairly complete, but have now collapsed inwards. Her position is 51 08 58; 01 28 17E and she is 5m proud in 23m.

230 U-16. It is perhaps poetic justice that one of the ships which sent her to the bottom should also lie on the seabed not far away. HMS *Cayton Wyke* (see Site 229) and HMS *Puffin,* patrolling the replica of the Dover mine barrage of 1918, depth charged *U-16* out of existence when they spotted her preparing to go through the barrage of 10 000 mines laid in the first 2 months of World War Two. In fact, in October three coastal U-boats, *U-12, U-40* and *U-16,* fell victim to the new barrage. As a result of these quick losses, the Germans sent all their U-boats north round Scotland to get their submarines into the Western Approaches to the Channel.

U-16 had a very short War, but did manage to sink two ships, the Swedish steamer *Nyland* and the French steam trawler *Ste Clair.* On this mission the U-boat was commanded by Kapitanleutnant Horst Wellner, who had previously commanded *U-14* in the Baltic, but was now part of the Johann Lohs Flotilla of the German submarine service (the flotillas of U-boats were all named after World War One German U-boat aces). He stopped transmitting on October 24, 1939, which is not surprising as HMS *Cayton Wyke* and HMS *Puffin* caught her that day in more or less shallow water and depth charged her until oil and air gouts suggested that she was finished. There is some reason to believe that some of her crew survived the actual depth charging as several days later the bodies of German sailors were washed ashore near Hythe – all were wearing Draeger submarine escape apparatus.

Today *U-16* is at 51 09 05; 01 28 12E. She was a small coastal U-boat, commissioned in 1935, 329 tons,138ft long with a beam of 13ft. She carried six torpedoes for her three bow tubes, and her 2cm gun was mounted immediately astern and almost part of the conning tower. There were 29 in her crew. She is upright on a flat seabed at 25m and 6m proud. Divers in 1984 noted that her hatches were open, but put that down to salvage operations which had clearly been carried out on her. They also reported that her stern was starting to deteriorate, though whether that outer casing damage was due to the depth charges they could not tell.

231 Unknown. At 51 09 15; 01 30 31E. A wreck well sunk in and standing only a little over 1m in 27m, with a scour adding another 2m. Echo distortion suggests a freshwater spring close by.

232 Unknown. At 51 09 18; 01 32 36E. Stands 4m proud of a very bumpy seabed at 27m. More diving information needed.

233 Stranded unknown, but only unknown until proper research is done! This one, at 51 09 16; 01 23 59E, is in only 2m and the wreckage stands 1m out of the sand at Coney Burrow Point, almost directly under the Dover Patrol Memorial. She was first charted in 1978.

234 Olympia. A British sailing ketch, sunk in 16m on March 13, 1918. Her masts showed at low water soon afterwards at 51 09 24; 01 24 32E. Today she is almost completely broken and bits stand less than 1m up from 16m, where she lies in a trench of her own making on a sloping seabed.

235 HMS Saxon Prince. This armed trawler of 237 tons was reported to have disappeared in a storm off Dover on March 28, 1916. She had been on patrol off the South Goodwins for 4 days and was due to return to Dover. She is charted as 15.2m in a general depth of 23m. At one time this was thought to be the tomb of *B-2*, sunk on October 4, 1912, in a collision with the liner *Amerika*, but recent diving has proved it to be the grave of HMS *Saxon Prince*. It may well be that the storm was not responsible for her loss, for divers found that her stern was missing and it looks very much as though she struck a mine. Her position is 51 09 33; 01 25 48E. Her bell has been recovered.

236 Nancy Moran. An American tug of 452 tons, she was towing a barge called *Tetem Two* when a collision sank her at 51 09 37; 01 27 44E. Now she is completely smashed up and her wreckage is spread over a wide area more than 70yds north and south of what remains of her hull on a mainly flat gravel seabed in 24m.

237 HMS Lydian. An armed trawler of 244 tons, she sank after striking a mine on September 18, 1915, off South Foreland. The mine was one of 12 in a field laid by Oberleutnant Count von Schmettow in *UC-6* and which he said were laid in the afternoon of September 15, on the edge of the South Goodwins. But the Count's navigation may have been at fault – the minefield was nearer to South Foreland than the Goodwins. *UC-6* may have been generally shaken on that day, however, for she went aground after laying the minefield and only just managed to get off! Today the trawler is well broken, lies north-west to south-east and is 7m proud in 24m. Divers in 1988 positively identified her by her bell. Position: 51 09 39; 01 26 14E.

238 Bucket dredger. Not much detail on this one at 51 09 49; 01 26 30E, except that she is definitely there and divers report her to be upside down in 23m, standing 6m proud. No date available for her sinking, but she was first swept in October 1937.

239 Unknown, but a big wreck at 51 09 37; 01 32 38E in 28m. Local divers say this is the wreck of an old steamer, standing 5m proud. She is upright. The area is one of very strong tides, so much so that the sand has been scoured away to the chalk bedrock towards her stern. Her telegraph has been recovered, but gives no real clue to her identity.

240 Hosanna. A 97 ton British beam trawler which was posted missing on February 16, 1980, after she left Plymouth for Scheveningen on February 14. Her position of 51 09 45; 01 34 24E in 47m is only approximate and based on a search and rescue helicopter sighting of oil seeping to the surface.

241 L'Armandeche. A wooden French fishing trawler well sunk into the sand at South Sand Head's east side at 51 09 53; 01 30 37E. She grounded on the steep side, but sank on June 29, 1982, when towed off.

242 Unknown. Another victim of the east bank of the South Goodwins, this is also likely to be a fishing vessel. Certainly she is just 30ft long, lying on the edge of the bank at 51 09 54; 01 31 00E in 23m.

AREA 4:

Kingsdown, Walmer, Deal and the South Goodwins

Admiralty chart No.1828   **Ordnance Survey map 179**

This area runs from 51 10 00 to 51 15 00 and covers the coast from Hope Point in the south to just north of the remains of Sandown Castle, taking in Kingsdown, Walmer and Deal on the way. It includes the famous Downs anchorage and the South Goodwins. Divers who plan to dive wrecks on or near the Goodwins should read the Goodwins diving advice which follows later in this chapter.

The chalk cliffs dominate up to Walmer Castle, which is just south of Deal. After that the coast is low with flat lands behind the beach. Deal exists only because a base was needed to serve all the shipping anchored in the Downs – there was so much in the times of sail that this was the most important (and the most crowded) open sea anchorage in the world. When the south-west or west winds blew, the sailing ships would gather in the Downs waiting for fair winds to take them westward. They could be there for weeks and that is when the Deal boatmen, or hovellers, would act as supply ships or taxis.They carried Lord Nelson ashore on many occasions – to dine with Sir William and Lady Hamilton at the Three Kings! They also acted as rescue boats when gales blew, ripping ships from their anchors and driving them on to the Goodwins. In November 1703, just such a gale caused the loss of the Navy warships *Restoration, Stirling Castle* and *Northumberland* and in 1809 another sent the *Admiral Gardner* to add to the toll of the Goodwins (these are all now protected wreck sites and included in this book). They are, of course, but a few of the ships lost on the Goodwins – over 2500 are recorded – and were only found when they emerged from the sands, which are over 2 miles wide at their broadest and about 12 miles long.

Deal has another claim to fame apart from servicing the Downs and being of service to Lord Nelson in his service of Lady Hamilton – in Marine Road, south of Deal Castle, is a plaque claiming to mark the spot where Julius Caesar landed in Britain on August 25, 55 BC. His galleys undoubtedly did scrunch on the steeply sloping shingle somewhere around here, though the actual spot may well be under the sea today. Divers close in should keep their eyes open for one of his legions' Imperial Eagles!

The Downs was the examination point in World War One for all ships going

Looking south along the beach at Deal, with chalk hills in background.

through the Straits. Some idea of the size of the job and the reason for the Navy's use of all kinds of pleasure boats as "boarding vessels" in their Auxiliary Patrol (see Site 288 for example) comes when you see the figures for the years 1915-17 of ships both Allied and foreign examined – 121,707. At these times as many as 120 ships a day waited in the Downs for checking that they were not carrying War materials for Germany. However, the U-boats took little advantage of all these targets and HMS *Niger* (see Site 273) is one of the few examples of a torpedoing inside the Goodwins.

During World War Two the Downs contraband control was put into operation again, but when France fell the Downs came within range of German long-range guns on the French coast. Ten Deal fishing boats helped with the Dunkirk evacuation in World War Two. Three were lost.

The most prominent landmarks for Deal from the sea are the big gas-holder, which is three-quarters of a mile north-north-west of Deal Castle, and the 1000ft long pier. Walmer today has both an offshore and inshore lifeboat and the lifeboat station has a long record of saving crews from ships on the Goodwins.

The South Goodwins

The presence of the Goodwins has a big effect on the tidal streams, which in most other parts of the Channel off the South Coast are clearly east-going on the

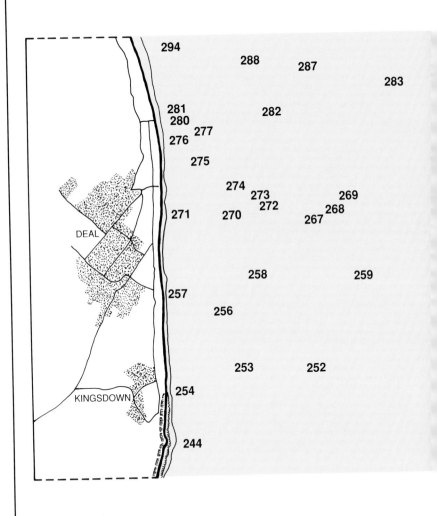

Dive Sites in Area 4

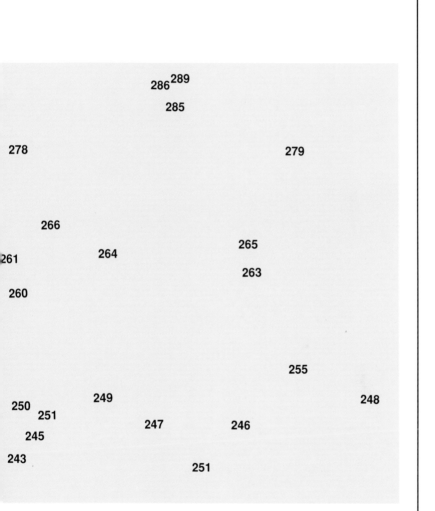

flood and west-going on the ebb. So in the Downs, and off the Kent coast between the south and north Forelands, the east-going is really north-going and the west-going becomes south-going. Inside the Goodwins that north-going stream can become violent towards the north-west. Diver cox'ns please note.

The southern part of the Sands is known as the South Calliper with South Sand Head at its southern tip. Don't take too much notice of charted depths around the Head for the area has huge sandwaves. The South Goodwin automatic lightfloat is at 51 08 00; 01 29 00E and is moored 2 miles south-south-west of South Sand Head. The South Goodwin lightbuoy is at 51 10 06; 01 32 04E.

The Kellett Gut is a through-passage between the drying parts of the Goodwins and for the purpose of this book divides the North Goodwins from the South. Be warned – the passage changes, which is why it is not much used by large boats. Take local advice! Take local advice too about the tides in the area. For example, the Admiralty warns that south of South Sand Head the north-going tidal stream near high water can run strongly towards and over the just-covered sands.

The amount of wreckage buried in the sands in this area is incredible. Richard Larn, who was much involved in the archaeological work on the *Admiral Gardner,* was a member of a team magnetometering the inner face of the South Calliper. He says that in 2 miles there was an anomaly every 50yds and each time the divers went down, they found ironwork, timbers, steel or other mixed wreckage. Not for nothing have the Goodwins become known as the Great Ship Swallower!

As the Goodwins sands are set on a chalk base, it seems likely, judging from divers' experiences with the *Stirling Castle, Northumberland* and *Admiral Gardner* – where they found the wrecks sitting on the hard chalk "bedrock" once the sand

Deal promenade, looking north, with Royal Hotel in foreground

had pulled away – that there may well be a whole layer of ancient and near-modern shipping sitting on that chalk base under the sand. When you remember that shipping has been lost on the Goodwins since the earliest times and that there are over 2500 recorded losses in there somewhere, just think of the sight if the sand all disappeared. What a wreck diver's paradise!

At the time of writing there is an unconfirmed report that yet another ancient wreck, complete and laden with bronze guns, has emerged from the Goodwins. Do not dismiss it as just another diving story. Ships have appeared without warning and been covered again just as swiftly, and more will emerge. Scientists now know that the Goodwins are real swingers. Aerial photography over the years has shown that the Sands pivot on Goodwin Knoll in the north and swing east for about 3 years – a distance of about 1000 yards. They then swing back to the west for another 3 years, rather like the pendulum of a big clock. So during the erosion ships will appear and during the build-up will disappear. This movement may have something to do with the fact that the Sands become unstable from the bottom up – a fact which makes the fate of shipwrecked sailors – thinking themselves safe on the apparently hard sand – all too certain, as the surface crust suddenly gave way beneath their feet.

Diving the Goodwins

Divers who have worked near the Goodwins stress that there must be no diving without bottom lines to anchor or shot. Many places on the inner faces are best dived at exactly low water slack, when dives can last for 40-60 minutes. There is, however, no substitute for local advice, which must always be heeded.

Visibility of 20m at total slack is not uncommon, but when the tide starts to run, the light fades fast. Within a few minutes, your buddy will disappear from sight as though the shutters have come down. A few more moments and you can hardly see your own hand. This loss of visibility happens so swiftly, particularly if a diver is engrossed in some wreckage, that bottom lines are absolutely essential. In less than 15 minutes the vis goes from 20m to zero. And the diver who has left it that long – too long – might find him or herself at the surface, with the tide boiling along at 4 knots. Goodwins diving is for very experienced divers only.

Launching sites

Kingsdown. Wooden ramp on front. To shingle. Parking nearby. Buoyed channel. Speed limit within 150yds of beach.
Deal. At north end of promenade, past the pier, are two concrete ramps for use at all states of tide. Speed limit within 150yds of beach, buoyed channels for water-skiers. Not always open in winter.

Diving sites

243 Santagata. This 7011 ton Italian motor vessel was loaded with phosphates when she grounded on the Goodwins on December 24, 1950. There was to be no Christmas present or happy ending for her – within a very short time she was broken in two almost equal parts at 51 10 27; 01 31 24E. Originally she had been 460ft long, with a beam of 60. Now the two halves are close together with the bow part lying to the north-east and the stern section to the south. The wreck is charted at 5.4m – this is the bow. The stern is the deepest part, in 18m.

244 The Wheatman. That's what they call her locally, but this is really the 1315 ton British steamer *Bellcairn,* built by Jackson and Cory in 1883 for Irvine and Co. The *Bellcairn* was 245ft long with a beam of 33ft and a draught of 16 and was driven by 130hp compound engines. She was bound for West Hartlepool from Sfax with a cargo of barley in October, 1894 when she was in a collision and sank close in off Kingsdown. Her cargo, swelling out of the steamer and washing up on the beach, gave her her nickname. Very broken in shallows near rifle range.

245 Agen. Engine failure in a gale put this French steamer of 4186 tons on the Goodwins on January 17, 1952. The 364ft long ship, which had a beam of 52ft and a draught of 24, and was loaded with mahogany tree trunks, broke in two in the huge seas. Divers who visited her recently at 51 10 42; 01 31 44E say that the two parts are now beginning to break up as well and low wreckage is scattered to the south-east of the main site, where the maximum depth of the wreck lying down a steep slope is 26m. Her highest point is 12m and sand is steadily covering her. Though wreck divers have taken many of her portholes, there are still others for those who are prepared to rummage amid the broken debris.

246 Unknown. A small wreck, possibly a fishing boat. At 51 10 50; 01 35 40E in 44m.

One of two concrete slipways at the north end of Deal promenade.

247 Le Pelerin de la Mer. Lies at 51 10 52; 01 34 00E in 45m after capsizing on October 18, 1980. Her crew were saved.

248 Unknown. At 51 11 07; 01 38 10E. Large steamer about 330ft long on a level sand and shell seabed at 41m, from which she stands 7m proud.

249 Unknown. At 51 11 07 ; 01 33 00E. About 260ft long with a beam of 49ft, this steamer lies on a flat bottom in 26m, from which she stands 6m proud. She has been swept, but is largely intact.

250 Luray Victory. An American steamer of the "Victory" type, which were built in the Liberty shipyards after 1944, 7612 tons, 455ft with a beam of 62ft and a draught of 38. She was on her way from Baltimore to Bremerhaven with a cargo of 3500 tons of oats and barley when she ran on to the Goodwins' South Calliper just before dawn on January 30, 1946. During the day the weather broke, a southerly gale came up and very soon the ship began to break up. The Walmer lifeboat dared huge seas to run alongside time after time to take off all the 49 crew. Today marks are not necessary to find her at 51 11 03; 01 31 38E as her two masts still stand up – one 9ft above high water and the other to the east dries 16ft. Most of the wreck is just 1m under, upright and full of sand, so much so that a recent dive on her found only the bases of the masts above the sand covering. Like most of this side of the Goodwins, the slope down to the east is very steep, and gets steeper as it goes further north along this edge.

251 Unknown. Only a little of this wreck now shows above the deep rippled seabed at 51 10 59; 01 31 50E and what is visible is very broken in just 7m. Metal detectors indicate a large iron content deep down, possibly cargo.

252 The Hulk. At 51 11 10; 01 27 18E. This is a wreck about 100ft long with a beam of 30ft, upright and lying north-east to south-west and 5m proud from 21m. You can swim in and out of her remains. Her engine is gone and she used to have a gun of World War One vintage.

253 Peter Hawksfield. This paddlesteamer with a cargo of coal lies at 51 11 11; 01 25 54E in 16m off Leathercoat and is 5m proud. Her bows are to the north-east and she is completely broken towards the stern so that a smaller part is now 75yds to the south-west.

254 Golden Sunset. A British fishing vessel which sank under tow just 200yds off Kingsdown beach on August 14, 1977. Her hull was filled with rubble to sink her completely and her mast and superstructure removed before she was left at 51 10 58; 01 24 30E some 300yds off the beach.

255 Unknown, at 51 11 28; 01 36 41E. A steamer very broken in 51m, standing 6m high on a flat seabed with her bows to the south-west.

256 Dolphin. Another paddlesteamer, which lies at 51 11 49; 01 25 26E. Some 70ft of her 197ft long hull still shows above the sand and stands 3m proud, lying toward the north-west, in only 7.6m. Built for the General Steam Navigation Co. in 1855, the 641 ton paddler could get 10 knots from her 180hp steam engines. On the night of September 18, 1885, she was doing a little less than that when she collided with the steamer *Brenda*. The *Dolphin* was towed by a tug into shallow water before she sank. Of the 25 passengers and crew she was taking from Dover to Le Havre, 5 were lost. Four of these were passengers, killed in their cabins by the impact of the collision which tore a great hole in her starboard side 30ft from her stern. In fact, she was struck with such force that she was cut nearly in two. This may account for the small part of her still visible.

257 Stranded unknown. Almost under Walmer Castle at 51 12 02; 01 24 27E, and drying. No definite identification, but could be one of three sailing ships – the *Georgia* (1861), the *Richard and Harriet* (1871) or the *Vega* (1880).

258 The Adjutant. At 51 12 12; 01 26 15E in under 10m are the remains of this steamer, which was subjected to prolonged dispersal operations in 1937-38. As a result little shows above the sand seabed.

259 Unknown. At 51 12 12; 01 28 15E. Charted as 18.1m in a general depth of 20m, this wreck is so sunk in that little stands higher than 1m.

260 North Eastern Victory. This 7176 ton former Victory type Liberty ship ran aground at speed in thick fog while coming from New Orleans to Antwerp with general cargo on December 24, 1946. When the lifeboat reached her she had already broken her back and the engine room was flooded. The crew of 36 were taken off but the Master and six officers stayed aboard. At dawn on Christmas Day the lifeboat was standing by again and as the ship was listing and clearly breaking up, the Master and his officers wisely decided to spend the rest of Christmas ashore. In 1960 four masts were clearly visible from Walmer and Deal. In 1976 only three masts stood and by 1991 there were only two. Today those two are still visible from shore. Her posi-

Excavation work on the Admiral Gardner, an East Indiaman which sank in 1809.

tion is 51 12 22; 01 31 24E. She is in two, with the minimum depth to her super-structure 3m and now only about a third of her shows above the sand. Her deck seems to be shearing away all round and if divers can find a way into her they should take great care not to become trapped by a sudden collapse.

261 Unknown. A small steel steamer about 90ft long at 51 12 44; 01 31 14E. No superstructure is left, but her bulkheads show. Divers found her full of sand, but her deck and bulwarks are clear to see. Highest point is her boiler, about 3m above general seabed level at 16m.

262 Admiral Gardner. Protected wreck with diving banned within 150m of 51 12 00; 01 30 56E under an historic wreck designation order which came into force on January 3, 1990. This is the second designation of the *Admiral Gardner*, which sank in 1809. The previous order, in 1985, became entangled in the different limits of Britain's territorial waters, but there is no doubt that the wreck was located by divers in 1983 after a fisherman snagged his nets.

The 800 ton *Admiral Gardner* was a British East Indiaman, outward bound in January 1809, captained by William Eastfield. Anchored off the Kent coast while waiting for a favourable wind, she got more wind than she wanted – a violent gale blew her, and her anchor, on to the Goodwins. She was not alone; two other Indiamen anchored near her now share her fate. The *Brittania* (see Site 266) and the *Apollo* hit the Goodwins nearby.

Archaeological diving teams found the *Admiral Gardner's* cargo of coins – East India Co. copper tokens, with face values in farthings. The native Indian workers were to be paid with them and they could only be cashed in the company stores. There were barrels and barrels of them. In fact, Dick Larn, the wreck researcher, who was one of the diving team, says that he believes there are probably still more than two million of the coins on the wreck – still in barrels, concreted in amongst a mass of cannon balls, tools, iron bars, nails, chain and other items of cargo. One hold, he says, is solid concretion in one lump about 50ft X 30ft and 15ft deep! And this is the only area which has been worked so far. That is not to mention the cannon, still attached to parts of their carriages amid massive timbers of the wreck, which is in three pieces.

263 Unknown. At 51 12 36; 01 35 54E. A small deep wreck which has been swept, she stands 8m up from a clay-sand seabed of 48m.

264 Silvio Onarato. An Italian steamer of 2327 tons ran on to the Goodwins at 51 12 53; 01 33 04E on January 2, 1948. Divers report her as reasonably intact, but deeply embedded. Her centre is full of sand so there is no way in.

265 Longhirst. Built in 1879 by Wigham Richardson and Co. with 204hp compound engines, this 2048 ton steamer was 285ft long with a beam of 36ft and was operated as a cargo carrier by Dunford and Elliott for many years. On June 6, 1901, she was in collision near the East Goodwin Light with the Norwegian steamer *Setubal* at 51 13 00; 01 36 00E while on her way from the Tyne to Barcelona with coal. Depth: 49m.

266 Britannia – possibly! Certainly this site at 51 13 08; 01 32 02E has been known for years to local fishermen as "The East Indiaman", and fishermen's tales have so often been proved right (see Site 262). Side-scan does show wreckage under the sand at this position and divers say that this is the wreck of a wooden ship which does cover and uncover. At the time of writing there is anything from 10-50ft over her!

267 Flandres. Belgian steamer of 5827 tons sunk in collision with another Belgian ship, the *Kablo* on February 12, 1940. This 422ft long steamer with a beam of 56ft and draught of 29 sank at 51 12 51; 01 27 21E. Sweeping in 1947 and 1959 has not been kind to this one – divers have found her well broken in 15m with her highest point a mere 2m at the stern. *Warning* – The stern is gill-netted.

268 Obstruction. Charted as 13.1m in 15m, this site at 51 13 00; 01 27 33E has apparently not been dived. Sonar has produced a small obstruction, but this is believed to be a freshwater spring.

269 HMS Tranquil. A War casualty, but as the result of a collision on June 16, 1942. This requisitioned trawler of 294 tons, built in 1912, sank at 51 13 08; 01 27 51E after hitting the motor vessel *Deal*. She lies north-west to south-east, 5m proud upright and surrounded by scours of her own making, taking the depth down to 17m. She is sometimes called the "Balloon Wreck" because when she was sunk she was towing a barrage balloon, used as part of a convoy's protection against air attacks, and after her sinking all that could be seen was the balloon attached to a cable which went under the surface of the sea!

270 Patria. At 51 13 01; 01 26 03E. A big ship, nearly 400ft long, deep in, showing 2m high in 10.5m. She has been well dispersed, but is worth a rummage. This is all that is left of the 5000 ton American liner, carrying 50 crew and 150 passengers. She caught fire well out to sea, but all aboard were safely transferred to other boats. The liner drifted, still on fire, to her present position where she sank. Attempts to raise her failed and she was dispersed.

271 James Harrod. This 7176 ton Liberty ship, built in Portland by the Oregon Ship Building Corporation in March, 1943, caught fire after colliding with another Liberty ship in the Downs, the *Raymond B. Stevens*, on January 22, 1945. As she was carrying a cargo of cased petrol and army lorries from New York to Antwerp, the fire raged until the 442ft long vessel was beached off Kingsdown. The crew were all saved by the daring of the captain of the Dutch coaster *Tromp* who put his ship alongside the blazing ship and took them off. Then a gale blew the *James Harrod* to the north until she finally stuck on the Malm Rocks almost under Deal Castle and broke in two.Surprisingly, thousands of cans of petrol and military vehicles were salvaged despite the fire. Burned-out lorries were dumped overboard and their remains can sometimes be found at the site.

The stern section was left at 51 12 59; 01 24 38E, but the fore part was towed to Sheerness in the hope of welding a stern section on to it. In April 1945 it was abandoned on Blythe Sands. Later it was refloated and laid up in the River Blackwater. In May 1946, the bow was towed to Bremerhaven, loaded with German gas weapons, towed to sea and scuttled. Now there is little to be seen near Deal Castle, but many a diving novice has scrabbled here in 3m of water on a first wreck dive!

Note – The *Raymond B. Stevens* survived the War and was scrapped in Philadelphia in 1961.

272 Jacob Luckenbach. This American steamer of 2793 tons, 322ft long, 39ft beam and draught of 22, is at 51 13 10; 01 26 33E. On July 5, 1916, she collided with the British steamer *Eddystone* while carrying a cargo of barley to Britain. Today she is very broken after sweeping in March 1981 and divers have found her highest point to be her condenser unit at 2m from the seabed in 14m. She is very close to wreck of HMS *Niger* (see Site 273).

273 HMS Niger. The first victim of Kapitanleutnant Walther Forstmann, who was to become Germany's second highest scoring U-boat ace with his two boats – *U-12* and *U-39*. *U-12* was the first U-boat to enter Zeebrugge on November 9, 1914, after the port had been captured by German troops. Two days later

Forstmann took her down Channel and found the old gunboat HMS *Niger* at anchor and totally unprotected off Deal Pier. He sank the *Niger* with a single torpedo.

The sinking caused a good deal of uproar. *The Times* reported it on November 12, 1914, under the heading of "Gunboat Sunk in the Downs. Torpedoed by a Submarine." The story read: "The Secretary of the Admiralty announced late last night: 'HMS *Niger* (Lt-Commander Arthur P. Muir, R.N.) was torpedoed by a submarine this morning in the Downs and foundered. All the officers and 77 of the crew were saved. Two men are severely injured and two slightly injured. There was no loss of life. HMS *Niger* was a torpedo-gunboat of 810 tons built in 1892. She was employed in semi-combatant duties.

'Thousands of people witnessed the sinking off Deal from the shore. There had been heavy gunfire all morning. About noon there was an explosion and columns of black smoke rose from *Niger,* which had been lying about 2 miles offshore just opposite the pier's head. A hundred boats were immediately launched, including the lifeboats from Deal and Kingsdown. Other boats put off from ships lying in the Downs. Deal lifeboat took off about six men and other boats the rest. About 20 minutes after the explosion the *Niger* went down very rapidly, her bows disappearing and the hull rising so that the greater part of her keel was visible and then she slid under.'"

Today the *Niger* lies at 51 13 12; 01 26 29E in 14m from which she is 3m proud and well broken with her bows to the north-east. Though at the time of her sinking she was described as a torpedo-gunboat, the 230ft long ship with a beam of 27 had been used as a minesweeper in 1909. She was armed with two 4.7in guns and four 3pdrs as well as three deck-mounted torpedo tubes. She had two funnels and her 3500hp engines could once produce 19 knots. Her wireless cabin was aft.

274 Brick barge. At 51 13 15; 01 25 48E. This is a small barge with her cargo of bricks still neatly stacked aboard. She lies to the north-west only 1.5m from flat seabed of hard sand at 12m.

275 Dinard. Small French steamer of 522 tons sunk at 51 13 34; 01 25 04E on December 7, 1939. She is now 2m proud in a mere 6m and not surprisingly divers of East Kent Maritime Trust described her in 1984 as "well broken up with the highest point 8ft above the seabed".

276 Africa. Was towed in and beached at 51 13 50; 01 24 43E after this British steamer of 1038 tons struck a mine on September 16, 1915, while carrying a deck cargo of railway carriages from London to Boulogne. Two crew were killed. The minefield had been laid by Oberleutnant Count von Schmettow in *UC-6* in the afternoon of September 15. Count von Schmettow reported that his mines were laid "on the edge of the South Goodwins – went aground while doing so, but finally got off", but there is considerable doubt about the position of this 12-mine field (see Site 237).

The *Africa* was broken up by explosives in 1917 and as a result is charted today as foul in 4m. Some claim this as one of the very few shore dives in Kent waters, but you'd need to be a strong swimmer to try it! A ship's bell recovered from the site is a very badly made iron affair.

Note – An amateur diver is reported to have found a 13in Roman amphora in

HMS Niger: sunk by an ace German U-boat commander in 1914. (See site 273.)

1972 amid the wreckage. Is the *Africa* lying on top of an ancient shipwreck or settlement? Or was her captain an antiques collector?

277 Nora. At 51 13 50; 01 25 10E are the remains of this Dutch motor vessel of 298 tons, which drifted ashore "1 mile east of Deal Coastguard" after being mined on January 29, 1940, while on her way from Harlingen to London. She almost demolished Deal Pier. She has been well dispersed, but is sometimes worth a rummage despite the shallow water. Her cargo was 317 tons of "strawboards".

278 Marauder. This twin-engined bomber is in 19m in Kellett Gut at 51 14 02; 01 31 29E, and is lying right on top of a very old wooden wreck! It was discovered by divers when searching for the wooden wreck after a fisherman had told of finding very old wood in his nets. Though the plane has not been positively identified as a Marauder, its twin engines, Browning machine-guns, and particularly its four-bladed props, each 15ft in diameter, make it unlikely to be an aircraft of any other type. The nose of the plane is either broken off or bent right under the body, which would indicate a violent landing on the sea except for the fact that all the propeller blades are perfect except for one on the starboard engine which is bent back about 18in from its tip. The number of .5 Browning cartridge cases under the wings and body are another indication that this is a Marauder, for these fast daylight bombers were nearly as heavily armed as the Flying Fortresses, carrying twelve .5 Brownings, including two in blisters on each side of the fuselage behind and below the cockpit. The skin on the wings is mostly intact, though the undercarriage wheels can be seen with big diamond-pattern tread on their tyres. The perspex of the rear turret is broken, but the guns are still there. There is some indication that this rear-gunner did not get out. Divers must treat this as a war grave.

The wooden wreck under the Marauder is clearly very old, with massive timbers of blackened wood, which are well sunk into the sand.

279 Unknown. At 51 14 00; 01 36 48E. A wreck of about 3-400ft long, standing 12m proud in 52m and lying north-north-east to south-south-west.

280 HMS Aragonite (stern). The tenth British warship to be sunk in World War Two, this armed trawler of 315 tons was completed in 1934. She was mined off Deal on November 22, 1939 and beached before she broke into two widely separated parts, both charted separately. Her stern section is at 51 14 08; 01 24 59E and is well sunk in around 4m.

281 HMS Aragonite (bow and midsection). This section used to contain her boiler, but in dispersal operations it was removed and dumped well out to sea. This part of her is at 51 14 14; 01 25 00E and is well scattered in 3m. Her crankshaft and pistons are clear to see, and despite the dispersal, a fine porthole was recovered in 1992.

282 British Navy. This 1216 ton sailing ship sank at anchor on November 26, 1881 following a collision with the iron-hulled *Larnaca,* which was also at anchor. The *British Navy* was bound from London for Sydney, Australia and was sheltering in the Downs from a violent south-easterly gale. When her anchor started to drag, Captain Skelly ordered out more chain. When she had 90 fathoms out she swung into the *Larnaca.* Captain Skelly, a pilot and 18 crew died when the *British Navy* sank. She is at 51 14 08; 01 26 31E. She was 216ft long with a beam of 35ft and was first dived in 1980. She is upright in 11m and 4m proud, but much broken. There is little doubt about the main part of her cargo for Australia – divers found her packed with blue and white china, mostly plates, cups and saucers. *Note* – The bell of the *Larnaca,* which didn't sink, was recovered by divers from the site and is now to be seen in Broadstairs' Bleak House Museum.

283 Mahratta. This is the first of two ships bearing the same name and both wrecked within a mile of each other, though 30 years apart. The first *Mahratta* was homeward bound from Calcutta for London and Dundee with 90 crew, 17 passengers and 10,000 tons of tea, jute, gum, rubber, rice and general cargo, and in the charge of a pilot when she went aground at 51 14 27; 01 28 52E on April 9, 1909, badly bending her prop shaft. Salvage of her cargo was successful, which is more than can be said for the efforts of nine tugs which literally pulled her in two at 9am on April 11! Despite the fact that she parted right across her middle, there was only one casualty – the Chief Engineer, Samuel Gibson, who slit his own throat for reasons no one has ever found out.

The 5730 ton *Mahratta* had been built in 1892 by Harland and Wolff and was operated by T and J. Brocklebank, a ship of 446ft, with a beam of 49ft and draught of 30, with 429hp triple expansion engines. Divers in 1984 found her well broken and thought that salvage operations were combining with the tide to flatten the wreck. In 1986 salvage of her pig iron ballast took place, but those divers reported the wreck intact apart from a hole blown in the port side, though they said that the superstructure was mostly gone. Least depth is 1m in 15m.

284 Mahratta II. Ran aground on October 6, 1939, while waiting for a pilot – less than a mile from the place where her namesake was wrecked 30 years before (see Site 283). The more modern *Mahratta* of 6690 tons was also owned by Brocklebank and was also homeward bound from India carrying a general cargo and passengers. Now she is at 51 14 45; 01 30 05E and 11m proud in 17m with a scour to the north of her as she lies east-west and a growing bank of sand to the south threatens to engulf her. The propeller and condenser are gone and some of her pig-iron ballast is spilling from her hull where the sides have collapsed. Massive surface swirls will help to pinpoint her.

The Goodwins often produce surprisingly good vis of over 20m. Divers on a recent visit to the *Mahratta II* were not only amazed to be able to see rows and rows of bales of jute, each 6ft long, lying in her open cargo holds, but when standing on the broken-off bow, now tilted upwards and pointing to the north-west, they found they could see both the dive boat on the surface and seabed below.

285 Ashley. A British collier of 1323 tons, 235ft × 35 × 14, she ran aground on the Goodwins on May 9, 1940, at 51 14 25; 01 34 29E while on her way from Sunderland to Southampton. This spot is close to the very steep fall-away of the Goodwins on their eastern side, dropping from nothing to over 30m in a matter of a hundred yards. Until very recently it was possible to see a small part of her superstructure at low tide, but now she seems to have sunk deeper and even diving on the outside slope has failed to reveal any trace of her.

286 Unknown. At 51 14 46; 01 34 15E. Wreckage charted as "foul" in 2m.

The Montrose: blown onto the Goodwins in 1914. (See site 290.)

287 Unknown. At 51 14 38; 01 27 14E. Charted as an obstruction, 82ft long with a beam of 23, standing 1m up in 11m, this one has not been dived, mainly because most informed opinion thinks it's a very large rock!

288 Marcella. A former pleasure yacht used as an armed boarding vessel of the Auxiliary Patrol, she was built in 1887 of 127 tons and sank on March 24, 1916, after a collision which badly damaged her stern. Now she is at 51 14 44; 01 26 08E, lying in 10m with her bow 5m proud and towards the east. Her superstructure has gone, but small guns fore and aft and an ammunition locker towards the damaged stern were still showing. Many coaster-size anchors are on her with their cables wrapped around parts of the wreckage, which is very silted.

289 Rynanna. Stranded on the Goodwins on January 23, 1940, at 51 14 52; 01 34 22E, this steamer is now a ship in a hole, none of her being higher than the general level of the seabed in 3m, though parts of her appear in a sandbank depression from time to time.

290 Montrose. May not be much of a dive, but will be for ever infamous as the ship in which Dr.Crippen, the wife murderer, disguised as a woman, tried to escape to the United States with his mistress. He was arrested on board by the ship's captain, following receipt of a shore to ship radio message – the first time radio had been used in this way. Crippen was returned to England where he was convicted and hanged in 1910.

The *Montrose,* of 7207 tons, a liner 444ft long with a beam of 52ft and draught of 28, was owned by Canadian Pacific until bought by the Ministry of War Transport in 1914 for use as a Dover Harbour blockship. She was filled with cement and made ready for scuttling when a mighty gale tore her from her mooring in the harbour and blew her across to the Goodwins, where at 51 14 56; 01 34 12E she foundered . Charted today as a stranded wreck, she dries about 3ft. The rest of her is in very shallow water and most of her lies under sand, although parts show in her own scour. The southern part of the wreck, her bow, is thought to lie over the wreckage of the *Rynanna* (see Site 289).

AREA 5:

Sandwich, Pegwell Bay, Ramsgate and North Goodwins

Admiralty chart No.1828   **Ordnance Survey map 179**

This area runs from 51 15 00 to 51 20 00 and covers the coast from the ruins of Sandown Castle to Ramsgate Sands, taking in Sandwich, the River Stour and Pegwell Bay. It includes the Small Downs anchorage, the Brake Sands, the Gull Stream, and the North Goodwins.

The actual coast and the countryside behind it is very flat, so much so that from the outskirts of Deal to the northern end of the Sandwich Flats it is all golf courses! The shingle gives way just north of Deal and, as you might expect from Sandwich, turns into sand dunes. A toll road runs to a large car park near the Prince's golf clubhouse, which gives access along the shore to the 700-acre nature reserve, the last untouched dunes and saltmarsh left in Kent. The Small Downs, an anchorage area to the north of The Downs, has always been a better anchorage for small vessels than its big brother. The Small Downs are more sheltered and the holding ground is better. The depth to the north of the Small Downs varies a great deal as there is a sandwave area pushing into it from the Brake, a very shallow area, which is not to be confused with another similar area, the North Brake, off Ramsgate. The Brake is the western edge of the Gull Stream, the route taken by most medium size ships passing from the Thames Estuary inside the Goodwins to the Channel and Western Approaches. The east side of the Gull Stream is the North Goodwins.

The northern tip of the Goodwins is North Sand Head and Goodwin Knoll. There are clockwise tidal movements in the area and local advice should be taken before diving. The North-East Goodwins automatic lightbuoy is at 51 20 00; 01 34 00E. Diving advice for the North Goodwins is the same as for the South (Area 4).

Sandwich Harbour

Admiralty chart No.1827   **Harbourmaster – tel: 0304 612162**
Sandwich is the furthest north of the Cinque Ports and the town today is 2 miles inland with 4½ miles of the twisting River Stour connecting it with the sea in

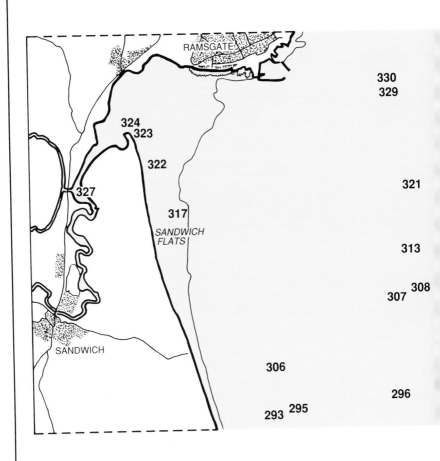

Dive Sites in Area 5

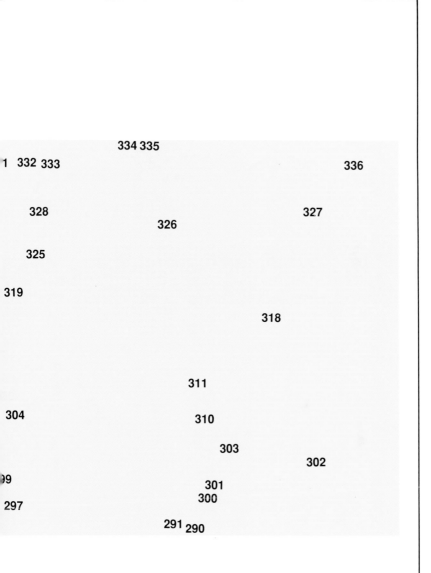

Pegwell Bay, about 2 miles south-west of Ramsgate. There are moorings at
Sandwich Quay and Sandwich Marina.

You can't miss the entrance to the river from out at sea. Just head for the
Richborough Power Station's chimney – 442ft high – and the three cooling towers nearby, which are a mere 337ft tall. In Pegwell Bay you enter an area of
extremely shallow water, which dries completely except for a narrow channel,
the outflow of the river. This channel is well marked with port and starboard
buoys at the seaward end and posts closer in. At Shell Ness you enter the river
proper. Here you can see the remains of two World War Two blockships which
closed off the river in 1940 in case of a German invasion. Crossing the bay, look
out for hovercraft. Their "flight path" is marked by spherical orange buoys.

Richborough Port is a short distance up the river. It is used today by power station ships, but in World War One was one of the main outlets used to ship munitions and railway rolling stock to France – 255 barges were towed back and forth
by tugs. After the War it became derelict and was almost forgotten. Just before the
outbreak of World War Two the port buildings were used to house 3500 Jews
fleeing from Nazi Germany. After these refugees were dispersed throughout
Britain, the camp became an army transit camp. Mulberry Harbour units were
built here for the Normandy landings of 1944 (see Site 10).

Pegwell Bay is also, by tradition, the landing place of Hengist and Horsa, the
Viking leaders from Jutland. They are said to have landed at Ebbsfleet. About 150
years later, in AD 597, St. Augustine followed on a mission to convert the pagans
of Kent to Christianity. A later Roman invasion by Claudius in AD 43 led to

Richborough Port, looking north-east towards Ramsgate.

Richborough Castle, or Rutupiae as the Romans called it, to become the first big Roman base in Britain and the chief port for the export of tin, lead, gold, silver, oysters, pearls, hides and grain. That is why divers in this area of Kent may well discover the first Roman or Viking wreck around the shores of Britain. So that you know what to look for, you should know that on a slope above the hoverport there is a replica of the Viking longship *Hugin,* which was sailed across the Channel by a Danish crew in 1949 to commemorate the 1500th anniversary of the landing of Hengist and Horsa. Of course in those times the Isle of Thanet really was an island and boats moved from Reculver in the Thames estuary through to Richborough without having to go round North Foreland.

Ramsgate Harbour

Admiralty chart No.1827   **Tel: 0843 592277**

Channel 14

Ramsgate itself is built around the harbour – or rather both harbours, because it has an inner harbour and an outer one, called Royal Harbour. An obelisk on the East Pier commemorates George IV's landing at Ramsgate in 1822.Today cross-Channel ferries and freighters bound for Dunkirk and other ports operate from a new Western Marine Terminal on reclaimed land to the south-west of Royal

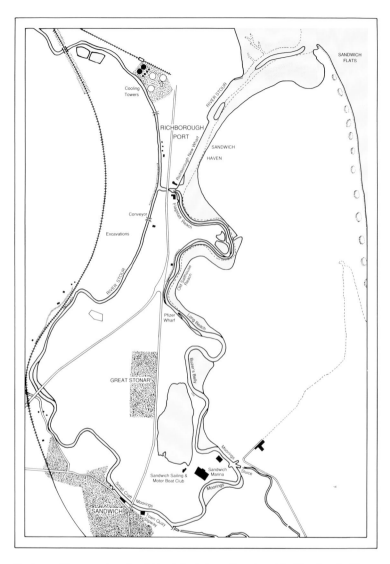

Harbour. Diver cox'ns should look for international port traffic signals (three vertical green lights for enter/exit; three reds for don't move) on a lattice tower
above a two-storey building about 70yds from the head of West Pier for both
the Western Terminal and the Royal Harbour entrances. These lights can be
difficult to see in bright sunlight. Diver cox'ns should also be aware of a strong tide
across the entrance, which produces an eddy off the head of the South Breakwater
and which can push boats on to the breakwater. When entering Royal Harbour aim

Above: Winterstoke Undercliff slip at Ramsgate. Opposite: Sandwich and Richborough.

to pass close to the west pierhead to avoid being carried east across or even past the entrance.

The inner harbour at Ramsgate is kept full by means of dock gates,which are normally open from about 2 hours before to 1 hour after high water. The inner harbour is really all marina, with 500 berths at floating pontoons. Ramsgate has both offshore and inshore lifeboats stationed in the outer harbour. In 1940, 82,000 men evacuated from Dunkirk were landed here.

There is no diving in any harbour without the special permission of the Harbourmaster – tel: 0843 592277. Divers visiting Ramsgate should make a point of going to the Maritime Museum at Clock House, right on the edge of the outer harbour, where they will find some first class wreck material. The museum is operated by the East Kent Maritime Trust. Check opening times by ringing 0843 587765.

Three miles west of Ramsgate is the RAF station at Manston, from which rescue helicopters are operated in liaison with HM Coastguards.

Launching sites

Sandwich. Concrete slip from town quay into River Stour. Can be used for 2 hours either side of high water. Speed limit of 6 knots in river.

Ramsgate Western Undercliff. At very end of esplanade, then down winding chine road to concrete ramp. Parking. (There is a charge.)

Ramsgate Harbour. Concrete slipway into inner harbour. Available at all times, but see details above of times of exit and entrance to Royal Harbour and sea.

Parking for car and trailer. There is an expensive launching charge and harbour dues are payable as well.

Ramsgate Winterstoke Undercliff, near East Cliff. Concrete slipway useable at all states.Parking for car and trailer.

Diving sites

291 Unknown. At 51 15 10; 01 34 03E. A large area of mostly buried wreckage charted as "foul" in 21m.

292 Kabinda. Great surface swirls and disturbance mark the site of the wreck of this Belgian steamer of 5030 tons and 412ft long with a beam of 52ft. She was carrying a cargo of maize when she grounded and broke her back at 51 15 03; 01 29 17E on December 10, 1939. Her crew of 44 were saved by the Walmer lifeboat. She lies with her bows to the north-east on a sloping seabed at 12m, though a 4m scour adds to that on her west side. The condition of this once intact wreck has changed greatly in the past few years and divers have now found that her highest point is just 3m under and she is breaking up badly.

293 Unknown. At 51 15 06; 01 25 11E. Her name ought to be known, for she was clearly visible in 1945 and was 441ft long, lying north-south with her upper deck, two masts and a funnel clear for all to see at all states of the tide. By 1959 nothing showed. Today small hummocks on the seabed in 6m standing 1m proud are the only signs of the ship. We do know that for years people said that this was the Liberty ship *Horace Binney,* which was beached at Deal after striking a mine in May 1945, but she was salvaged and finally scrapped in Antwerp in 1948.

294 Ilaro. A British merchantman of 2799 tons, 310ft long, beam of 40ft, and draught of 17, belonging to the Elder Dempster Line. She was mined on October 23, 1915, off Dungeness when on her way from Forcados, Nigeria, to Hull with a cargo of palm kernels and maize. One man was killed when the mine exploded and started a fire on board. Even so the *Ilaro* kept going and was well ablaze when she arrived in the Downs, where her captain finally had to beach her at 51 14 53; 01 24 39E in very shallow water. Today she is broken all over in 5m with the biggest part 3m proud.

295 A big rock, or could be. At 51 15 12; 01 25 35E, this is a natural feature of some kind standing 1m proud of a flat seabed in 9m and about 30yds in diameter.

296 Lancresse. A collision with the Norwegian steamer *Tres* on November 22, 1935 while she was on her way to Guernsey put the steamer *Lancresse* amid sandbanks at 51 15 21; 01 27 48E. Originally she was in a depth of 14m, but sand movements have now covered her so that the general depth is 4m, from which only a small part of her protrudes.

297 Piave. A blinding snowstorm on January 29, 1919 brought the maiden voyage of the 6000 ton American steamer *Piave* to an abrupt end when she stranded on the north-west edge of the Goodwins at 51 15 17; 01 30 20E. Registered in New Jersey, the steamer was loaded with food in New York to take to the starv-

The entrance to the inner harbour at Ramsgate.

ing people of Rotterdam, the survivors of the war which had just ended. Unfortunately, they were never to see the food for the first attempt to get the *Piave* off involved dumping overboard a thousand bags of flour and hundreds of sides of bacon and cases of lard. More and more food was flung into the sea in the next 2 days and fuel oil followed, but all efforts by tugs failed to shift her.

At 5.30pm on January 31, the ship suddenly parted amidships and her generators failed. At the same time she heeled violently and there was panic aboard, with a mad scramble for the boats, which were let slip and ended up hanging vertically. Men jumped overboard, some straight into the Deal lifeboat which was standing by. Amazingly, not a single man of the 96 in the crew was lost. The President of the United States presented the lifeboat cox'n, William Adams, with a gold watch and gave a gold medal to every member of the lifeboat crew, for the rescue. Today she is well sunk in but seems to be uncovering and is 2m proud in 16m.

298 HMS Northumberland. Protected wreck site. No diving within 50m of 51 15.45; 01 30.12E (position as given in the protection order of December 8, 1989). The Great Hurricane of November 27, 1703 struck the northern part of the Downs off Deal just when it was crowded with over 200 ships sheltering from the wild weather which had plagued the previous fortnight. Ship after ship was ripped away and for those that missed the Goodwins, the Brake Sands were an unwelcome alternative. The men o' war in the anchorage fared no better and when the storm reached its height around 3am, some of the really big ships were torn away from their anchors. *Northumberland,* a third rate of 70 guns, was thrown on to the Goodwins and Captain Greenaway and all her 253 crew died. *Restoration,* another third rate, commanded by Captain Fleetwood Emes, hit the Goodwins close by and not one of the 386 aboard survived. *Stirling Castle* hit the Goodwins further to the north and 70 of her crew of 349 were saved.

The *Northumberland* was discovered by divers after a fisherman got his nets caught – and they found themselves facing a complete 18th century ship poking out of a giant sandbank. They could even lift the gunport lids and swim inside down rows of guns! The ship had clearly just emerged due to some movement of the Goodwins, but it didn't stay intact for long. Her sudden exposure was too much for her and she is now largely collapsed. Archaeologist in charge is Dr. Mark Redknap.

299 HMS Restoration. Protected wreck site. No diving within 50m of 51 15.60; 01 30.12E (position as given in protection order of December 8, 1989). This is just 270yds north of the *Northumberland* and so far the site has only been investigated by sonar, which shows her wreckage both under and above the seabed. Similar soundings off South Calliper have shown a possible 15th-16th century site, from which area an early composite stave-built swivel gun, still on its oak bed, has been recovered. It is now in the Royal Armouries at the Tower of London.

300 Unknown. At 51 15 28; 01 34 35E. Something 62ft long and 29ft wide is here and charted as "foul" in 10m. It is an area of big sandwaves.

301 Two unknowns. At 51 15 33; 01 34 43E. The bigger of the two is 272ft long with a beam of 65ft. Close by – 200yds south-west – is the other, 62 × 29. Both are 1m proud of the seabed at 9m.

302 East Goodwins Light Vessel. She was Light Vessel No.54 and was sunk by German bombers on July 18, 1940. Fortunately this was after Trinity House had demanned all light vessels following German attacks on the East Coast ships. She is now 6m proud in 46m, lies north-south, and her position is 51 15 49; 01 36 46E.

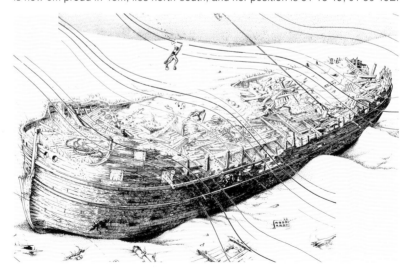

Wreck of the Stirling Castle, a victim of the Great Hurricane of 1703.

303 Unknown. At 51 16 00; 01 34 59E. A steamer, very broken in 14m, lying north-south, about 100ft long, but with much buried.

304 HMS Stirling Castle. Protected wreck site. No diving within 50m of 51 16.426; 01 30.516E (position as given in the amended protection order of September 30, 1980). Another victim of the Great Hurricane of 1703 (see Sites 298 and 299) and another fisherman's nets becoming snagged led to Thanet BSAC divers discovering her in June 1979 in 23m. It was clear that the sands were moving back from her – the charted depth at that time was just 4m – and as they did so the Thanet divers found themselves confronted with a more or less intact ship some 8m high, 151ft long with a beam of 40, embedded in a cliff of sand. They swam into her through the gun ports and surveyed the 40 of her 70 cannon which they could reach and raised one bronze cannon captured from the Dutch and overstamped with the Navy's broad arrow. Of the ship's masts there was no sign – nor would there be, for the *Stirling Castle* cut down her masts in a vain attempt to stop being driven on to the Goodwins by the huge winds. In all the diving team of John Cayser, Roy Kennett, Paul Fletcher, Paul Hale, Keith Young and John Chamberlain, who carried out the first archaeological work on the wreck, raised some 300 small items of pewter, stoneware, and personal possessions of the crew, only 70 of whom survived out of the 349 aboard when she struck on November 27, 1703. Divers can see many of those recoveries in the Maritime Museum at Ramsgate in the Clock House, Royal Harbour. Archaeologist in charge of the protected site is Dr. Mark Redknap. Since being exposed by the sand, the wreck of the *Stirling Castle* has collapsed and sand is encroaching once again.

305 La Nantaise. Despite the name, this is a British steamer of 359 tons which sank after a collision with the s.s. *Helencrest* on July 8, 1945. She has been swept but is still mainly intact, and upright, in 10m. Sand covers most of her, but varies from year to year. She is at 51 16 30; 01 29 02E.

306 HMS Napia. A British tug of 155 tons, built in 1914 and hired for the examination service of shipping on December 6. 1939, soon after the outbreak of World War Two. She stayed in her job just 14 days, as she was mined "off Ramsgate" on December 20. She was dispersed in 1959 and is now spread over the seabed at 6m in an area of about 50 square yards. Nothing stands more than 1m proud at 51 15 41; 01 25 11E.

307 Koenigshaven. Though she was lost during World War One – on February 2, 1917 – it was the weather that put her on the bottom at 51 16 38; 01 28 03E. This 1245 ton Norwegian steamer, 280ft long with a beam of 59ft, carrying a cargo of coal from Newcastle to Rouen, sprang a leak and foundered in a storm. Afterwards her funnel and masts could be seen for some days, but today, after numerous sweepings over the years, she is broken in two with one part dragged 500ft from the other and in 13m on a generally flat seabed. Both parts are about 3m proud. The most westerly part of the wreck points north-west and has a 1m scour, the easterly section lies east-west and has a scour all around it.

308 Malta. A bit of a mystery ship. We know her name and her size – 190ft with a beam of 56ft. We know that HMS *Daisy* reported a dangerous wreck with her masts sticking up out of the water on March 12, 1917 somewhere very close to her present position of 51 16 39; 01 28 13E, but she doesn't seem to have left a record of how she got there. Today she is 5m proud in 13m, upright and swept.

309 Unknown. At 51 16 17; 01 29 30E. This old steamer is on a very steep slope on the edge of the main sandbank, 190ft long with a beam of 49, and just 4m under at her highest point.

310 Unknown. At 51 16 23; 01 34 27E. Steamer lying with her bow to the south-east, broken almost in half. There is a 2m scour on her north side, but general depth is 16m from which she stands nearly 5m proud. She is about 360ft long with an estimated beam of 65.

311 Lord Hamilton. A 64 ton barge lost on February 14, 1924, when she grounded on the north-east edge of the Goodwins. She is now at 51 16 52; 01 34 19E, broken, but 2m proud in 19m.

312 Egero. Sunk in the Gull Stream after a collision on March 4, 1916, this Norwegian steamer of 1373 tons was 245ft long with a beam of 34ft and a draught of 16. Today she is at 51 17 06; 01 29 04E, lying north-east to south-west in 14m with a 2m scour on her southern side. She has been dispersed, but is still over 2m proud in places.

313 Mersey. A British steamer of 1037 tons, she was mined near the Midbrake Buoy on April 20, 1940, as she was carrying 650 tons of general cargo, plus some iron and steel, and 350 tons of sand from Antwerp for Goole. Captain W. Rocket and 13 of his 20 man crew were killed. A former London, Midland and Scottish Railway steamer, she was built in 1906 by Swan Hunter and Wigham Richardson with 342hp triple expansion engines which could give her 14 knots. Now her position is 51 17 10; 01 28 09E and this 255ft long ship with a beam of 36ft and draught of 16 is very broken in 12m and spread over a wide area with her highest point 2m proud.

314 Unknown. At 51 17 24; 01 29 45E. A steamer emerging from the sand and lying on the ridge which once covered her. She is 4m proud in 12m. She is about 245ft long, is well broken after sweeping and lies east-west.

315 U-48. At 51 17 06; 01 29 48E. Commanded by Kapitanleutnant Carl Edeling, this was a big boat of the Mobilization-class, 213ft long, with four bow tubes and two stern and of 940 tons. With a crew of 36, she left Wilhelmshaven on November 21, 1917, to attack shipping in the Western Approaches. She could do over 15 knots on the surface, but was spotted when 60 miles from Dover and bombed, but not hit, by a seaplane. Edeling dived and waited for dark to start his run through the Straits. His compass failed and the strong westerly tide carried him on to nets off the North Goodwins which entangled his propellers. At 3am on November 24 he stranded on the Goodwins. Despite jettisoning 60 tons of oil fuel, fresh water, gun ammunition and 3 torpedoes, he could not free the sub from the bed she had made for herself in the sand and the ebbing tide put her more firmly in.

At dawn she was spotted by the trawler *Meror* patrolling to the south and at the same time by two Ramsgate drifters, *Majesty* and *Paramount*, who had been sweeping the War Channel to the north-west. Then three more drifters, *Present Help, Acceptable* and *Feasible,* appeared. A gun battle between the drifters' six-pounders and the submarine's 4.1-inch gun was short and sharp and finished when the drifters closed in and were joined by the old destroyer HMS *Gipsy.* Several of the U-boat's gun crew were killed. Carl Edeling was seen to be badly wounded in the head. When the submarine caught fire, he ordered her to be blown up. The crew jumped into the water, but Edeling and 18 men were not picked up.

U-48 comes out of the sand from time to time.She was seen in 1921, and again in 1939. Her most recent appearance was in June1973. The reports of this happening in the British press brought a letter from Carl Edeling's son in Essen pointing out that the sub had reappeared 70 years to the day after his father entered the German Navy.

316 Unknown. A bank of sand has rolled over this 210ft long steamer with a beam of 56ft, and at the present time there is very little to be seen of her. She is charted as swept 13.4m in a general depth of 14m. However, there are signs of more of her appearing at 51 17 03; 01 29 23E.

317 Lancaster bomber. This aircraft shows a propeller blade at low tide, but most of the rest of her is still there at 51 17 40; 01 23 12E. This "Lanc", returning from a 1000 bomber raid on Germany, was badly damaged and ditched in Pegwell Bay in 2m of water. Air-sea rescue helicopter crews say her whole outline can be seen from high above.

318 Unknown. A very small one, about 42ft long, lying north-east, south-west, or part of a bigger ship. The wreckage lies at 51 17 40; 01 35 50E. It is 3m proud in a depth of 20m.

319 Brighton Belle. A paddlesteamer of 396 tons, 200ft long with a beam of 24ft and a draught of 8ft. She was requisitioned by the Admiralty for use as a minesweeper at the outbreak of World War Two, because the Navy remembered how useful these shallow-draught paddlers had been against mines in World War One. The *Belle* had been used then too, as she had been built in 1900. There are conflicting reports about how she met her end at 51 18 00; 01 30 25E on May 28, 1940 – the one which would put her in the correct spot says that she hit a sunken wreck and sank there. However, a Lloyds report says that she was lost at Dunkirk during the evacuation "about May 31". The two are not impossible to combine – the evacuation of British troops from Dunkirk, "Operation Dynamo", started in the afternoon of May 26. Perhaps the paddlesteamer was going, or had already been, to Dunkirk when she sank, or possibly she has been con-fused with the other Brighton paddlesteamer, the 807 ton *Brighton Queen,* which was indeed lost by gunfire off Dunkirk on June 1. Today she lies in 11m, is very broken after dispersal and is 2m proud of a big scour which takes the maximum depth to 15m.

320 Brendonia. She was a 313 ton collier and was loaded with Tyne coal for Italy when the weather put her on the Goodwins on September 11, 1939 at 51 17 54; 01 29 44E. She lies completely within her own scour which takes her 2m below the seabed of 11m and appears largely intact, though much of her is under sand.

321 Unknown. At 51 17 59; 01 28 07E. A small wreck standing 1m proud of 11m and very broken.

322 Stranded Unknown. At 51 18 18; 01 22 46E. Not a dive as such, but mentioned here because she is sometimes used as a mark. This is a 42ft long vessel constructed of wood and iron, mostly buried in sand, but with her bow the highest point.

323 HMS Harvest Moon. This one – an Admiralty requisitioned trawler of 72 tons, built in 1904 – and HMS *Alfred Colebrook* were sunk on September 9, 1940, as part of the defences against a German invasion across the Channel. They were blockships to close off the River Stour. The trawler shows clearly at low water at 51 18 45; 01 22 07E and dries nearly 5m.

324 HMS Alfred Colebrook – a 56 ton requisitioned drifter built in 1912 – was sunk in the "Richborough Channel" on the same day as the *Harvest Moon* (see Site 323), as part of England's defences against the expected German invasion. Her position is 51 18 47; 01 22 08E. She dries about 5m but is only recognisable as a mass of tangled pipes.

325 Bravore. When this Norwegian collier carrying 1993 tons of coal from the Tyne to Rouen was mined a mile south of Gull Buoy on April 22, 1940, 14 of her crew and 4 French naval ratings were lost. She was an old ship, built in 1916 by Kockums M/V with 156hp triple expansion engines and operated by A/S Vore. She was 235ft long with a beam of 38ft and draught of 16 and of 1458 tons. Divers have found her widely dispersed in 12m, with nothing standing higher than 1m at 51 18 30; 01 30 51E.

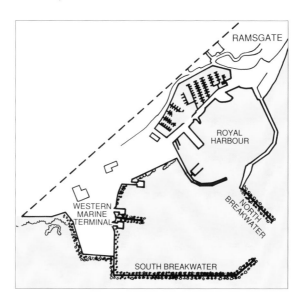

Above: the inner harbour at Ramsgate. Opposite: Ramsgate Harbour.

326 Unknown. At 51 18 51; 01 33 38E. A very small wreck or a piece ripped off another one, standing only half a metre high in 15m.

327 Unknown. At 51 18 59; 01 36 38E. She is about 127 ft long, standing 5m proud in 18m.

328 Rydal Force. A small British collier of 1101 tons, carrying 1250 tons of coal from Sunderland to Cowes, she was mined 400yds south of the Gull Buoy on April 24, 1940. Eleven men died in her sinking. Now she lies at 51 19 02; 01 30 59E in an area of sand waves. She only just shows above the general seabed level of 9m and is in a deep scour.

329 Neg Chieftain (part of). This Panamanian tug overturned on August 10, 1983, while towing the barge *Stonecarrier,* which also capsized. The accident was due to one of the barge's towing chains parting while she was heading for Ramsgate. In January 1985 the wreck of this tug was raised by the crane-barge *Taklift One,* but part of her was left behind at 51 19 14; 01 27 42E in 3m of water.

330 Stone Pile. At 51 19 20; 01 27 38E. This is where the barge *Stonecarrier* dropped the 2500 tons of stone she was carrying during the *Neg Chieftain* accident (see Site 329). The stone pile stands 1m high in 5m.

331 Harcalo. A British steamer of 5081 tons, 418 × 56 × 24, which was carrying 7500 tons of iron ore from Benisaf to London when she was mined on June 6, 1940. Three of her crew of 39 died. She was beached north-west of the Gull

121

Riverfront at Sandwich, near the Town Quay slipway.

Buoy at 51 19 36; 01 30 12E and lies east-west in 7m on a steep bank from which part of her is 3m proud. She is broken in two about 90yds apart.

332 Merel. A British steamer of 1088 tons built in 1925 at the Ayrshire Dockyard Co, with 298hp triple expansion engines which gave her 11 knots. Commanded by Captain Wastell, she was on her way from Le Havre to London with 1000 tons of general cargo including brass rods, aniline and casein, when she was mined off the Gull Buoy and sank at 51 19 37; 01 30 49E on December 12, 1939. Her captain was among the 16 killed out of a crew of 18. She was 246ft long with a beam of 36ft and draught of 12 and was owned by the General Steam Navigation Co. at the time of her loss. Today she is in two pieces about 40yds apart due to sweeping. The northern part of her is charted at 8.9m on a wildly undulating seabed at a mean depth of 11m. Sand appears to be starting to cover the northern section.

333 HMS Arctic Trapper. Attacked and sunk by German aircraft on February 3, 1941, this ship was an Admiralty requisitioned trawler of 352 tons built in 1928. Now she lies on the northern slope of a ridge in 11m with a scour of 1m on her northern side. She is well broken and stands at most a metre proud at 51 19 37; 01 31 07E.

334 HMS Elizabeth Angela. Attacked and sunk by German aircraft on August 13, 1940, this 253 ton trawler was requisitioned by the Admiralty for minesweeping in 1939. In the air attack one of her crew was killed before she sank in shallow water with her mast still showing. Now she is still there – at 51 19 51; 01 33 05E – 3m proud and on the edge of a bank in 12-14m. Sand tends to cover and uncover parts of her, but the whole of her stern appears to be missing. There are a number of shell cases on the wreck.

335 Correct. "Lost by enemy action" in February 1916, is the only record I can find of the end of this 230ft long steamship. Strangely, she does not appear in any of the main official records of ships lost by enemy action during World War One. She may have been a very late victim of a drifting wartime mine, for a ship of that name in the right area appears to have sunk in 1920, or at any rate to have been dispersed in June 1920 at 51 19 51;01 33 14E. She was dived in 1984 by sport divers who described her then as in 13m, well broken, with her stern the largest part of her remaining intact and upright 2m proud.

336 Dutch schooner. At 51 19 37; 01 37 40E. This was one of the Dutch ships which escaped when Holland was overrun by the German panzers in May 1940. No details of her sinking can be found but she hit the bottom on May 30, 1940. She is now in 24m, from which her 200ft long hull stands 7m proud and lies north-south. Diving details needed.

Wooden slipway inside the harbour at Broadstairs, with Bleak House in the background.

AREA 6:

Broadstairs, North Foreland and Margate

Admiralty chart No.1828   **Ordnance Survey map 179**

This area runs from 51 20 00 to the top of chart 1828 at 51 25 03. It covers Broadstairs, North Foreland, Foreness Point and Margate.

Broadstairs is only 1¼ miles north of Ramsgate and has the shallow Broadstairs Knolls as the outermost shallow patches on the flats which run out from the coast between Ramsgate and Broadstairs. Broadstairs Knoll Buoy is moored off the east side at 51 20 08; 01 29 06E.

Divers may find a visit to Bleak House at Broadstairs interesting, even if they are not Dickens fans. Bleak House has a deal of wreck material as it is also the Maritime Centre.

The sheer cliffs of North Foreland, rising to 121ft, mark the entry to the Thames Estuary. A conspicuous octagonal tower, 85ft high, is the lighthouse, close to the edge of the chalk cliffs. There is a shallow sandy ridge running out from North Foreland. It ends at the Elbow, where the Elbow lightbuoy is moored, at 51 23 02; 01 31 07E. From North Foreland to Margate the coast is mostly cliffs with rocky ledges jutting out to sea. Largest of these is Longnose Ledge which dries out at low tide and runs for 1,000yds out from Foreness Point. The chalk gullies look ideal hunting grounds, but there are two sewer outfalls there!

Margate has always been London's beach playground, hence the funfair and amusement arcades. There is a small harbour which dries out and shelters behind Stone Pier. An offshore and an inshore lifeboat are stationed at Margate.

Launching sites

Dumpton Gap. Steep track down to concrete ramp and sand.Large boulders at foot of ramp make launching difficult at any time other than high tide.

Broadstairs Harbour. Admiralty chart No.1827. A concrete and a wood slipway are useable for 2 hours either side of high tide. Speed limit 5 knots inside harbour and 8 knots inshore.

Palm Bay. Near Foreness Point. Concrete slipway at all states. Parking.

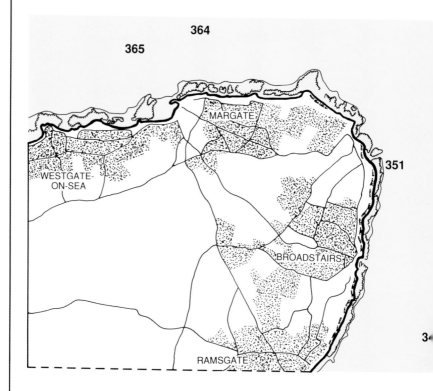

Dive Sites in Area 6

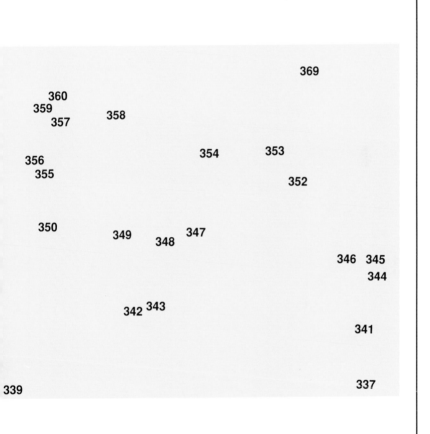

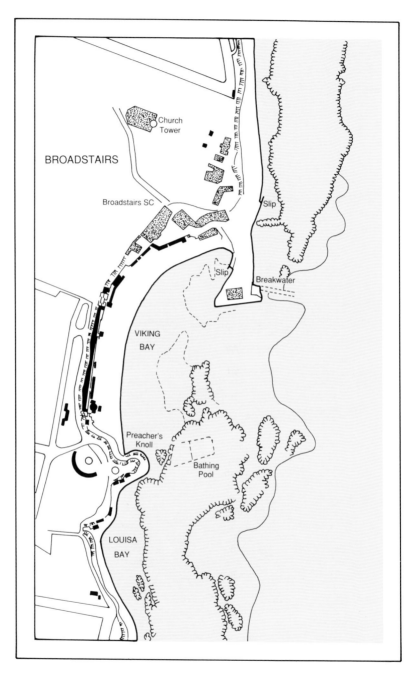

Above: Viking Bay, Broadstairs. Opposite: Broadstairs, showing inner and outer slips.

Margate Harbour. Admiralty chart No.1827. Concrete slips useable 2 hours either side of high tide.

Diving sites

337 Liberator. This B-24 American bomber lies upside down at 51 20 04; 01 30 05E. She has her wheels down – which in this case means up! – and the tyres are still inflated. It is possible that she was trying to land at nearby Manston during World War Two. The Liberator bomber had a wing span of 110 feet and the deep fuselage was 63ft long with gun turrets in nose and tail. She could carry 8000lb of bombs and a crew of 6 men. She lies with her nose to the north-west in 19m and the top of her tyres are nearly 4m proud.

338 Greypoint. A small steamer of 894 tons, she was unlucky to cross the path of a German torpedoboat-destroyer on March 18, 1917, 2 miles off Broadstairs, and was promptly torpedoed. Today she lies in 10m and very broken at 51 20 20; 01 29 30E.

339 UB-12. This early UB-class boat of World War One was the only one of these small attack boats converted to carry mines. She had eight mines and no torpedo tubes and only a machine gun for defensive or offensive action. She was 92ft long and had claimed 21 ships as victims of her mines with a total of 10,142 tons by the time she set out from Zeebrugge on August 19,1918.

Commanded by Oberleutnant Ernst Schoeller, the orders were to lay her mines in the "northern exit of the Downs". Nothing more was heard of her and there were no survivors from her crew of 14. What is thought to be her wreckage is at 51 20 04; 01 30 05E and is protruding from the edge of a sandbank. It is believed that this 142 ton boat was a victim of her own mines as there was no British minefield in the area.

340 Unknown. At 51 20 24; 01 28 17E. A very small wreck, about 7m long in 7m and 2m proud.

341 Alert. A small British cableship of 941 tons, carrying out repairs to cables for communications with Allied forces in France, she was destroyed in an enormous explosion on February 25, 1945 "off North Foreland". Official records of what happened to the 196ft long ship with a beam of 31ft and draught of 20 are not definite – "presumed torpedoed by a U-boat or midget submarine, or possibly fouled an old mine" – but all the crew of 54 and 6 gunners were lost. No U-boat commander claimed the *Alert,* which today lies very broken in 18m at 51 20 44; 01 37 40E from which she stands only 2m high.

342 Klar. A small Norwegian collier of 518 tons laden with 590 tons of coal and coke, she was travelling from the Tyne to Rouen, when she was mined on November 27, 1915, at 51 21 03; 01 32 49E. She was 150ft long with a beam of 25ft and draught of 17 and is now very broken and scattered in 12m. There is another wreck very close by. (See Site 343.)

343 Yvonne. This Belgian steamer of 668 tons was bound from London for Cardiff with a cargo of cement when she hit a mine and sank at 51 21 06; 01 32

Broadstairs Breakwater, looking towards outer slip and North Foreland.

The 10,000-ton liner Dunbar Castle: sunk off North Foreland in 1940.

48E on June 12,1940. Of her crew of 12, only 2 survived. It is likely that her wreckage is entangled with the *Klar* (see Site 342) and included in the area charted as "foul".

344 Unknown. At 51 21 25; 01 37 51E. Steamer wreck in 19m about 100 ft long with a beam of 25ft, standing upright and 7m proud, north to south.

345 Unknown. At 51 21 37; 01 37 54E. Small wreck about 65ft long in 20m and 4m proud.

346 Unknown. At 51 21 38; 01 37 17E. Small steamer about 80ft long, 3m proud in 22m.

347 Cathy. A Danish steamer of 4076 tons, 369 × 47 × 18, mined on May 5, 1915, while on voyage from Copenhagen via Newcastle for Singapore with general cargo. Today she is in two parts at 51 22 00; 01 34 25E, the highest part standing 3m proud in 14m. The more southerly section is almost entirely covered by sand.

348 Unknown. At 51 21 54; 01 33 30E. Another small wreck, wire swept to seabed level at 12m and so broken that it is charted only as "foul".

349 HMS Frons Oliviae. This Admiralty-hired trawler of 98 tons was sunk after hitting a mine on October 12,1915. The mine was part of a field laid by Oberleutnant Pustkuchen in *UC-5*. Now his victim lies at 51 22 02 ; 01 32 34E, upright though swept, in 12m and 2m proud. Her bow is to the north-east.

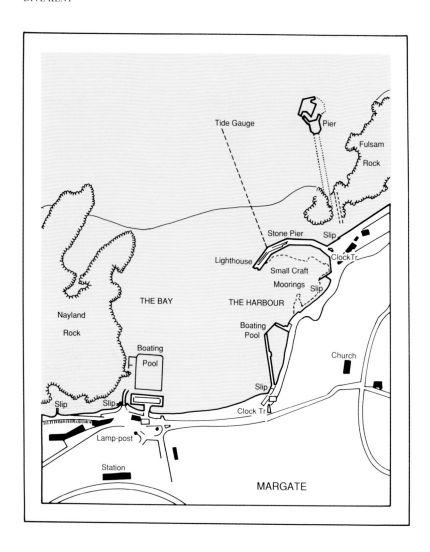

MARGATE

350 Lolworth. Another mine victim, this British steamer of 1969 tons was heading from Portsmouth for the Tyne in ballast when a mine exploded under her bow. Two of the crew of 22 died in the explosion on April 23,1940. Today the 270ft long ship, which had a beam of 40ft and a draught of 17, lies at 51 22 07; 01 30 59E. She was dispersed in 1961 and as a result is very broken in several sections, the tallest of which is only 1m proud in 9m.

351 Obstruction. At 51 22 36; 01 27 20E. Standing 1m proud in 3m. Recent diving suggests it may be sanded over since first reported in 1979.

Above: Margate Bay, viewed from the Lifeboat Slip. Opposite: Margate Harbour.

352 Dunbar Castle. A magnetic mine dropped by a German aircraft exploded right under the bridge of the 10,002 ton liner on January 9,1940, when she was outward bound from London to Beira and southern Africa as part of a convoy. On board the 471ft long ship with a beam of 61ft and draught of 29, were a crew of 150 and 48 passengers. The 4400 tons of general cargo included automatic scales, spoons, gin and salted herrings. Captain H.A. Causton, on the bridge, was fatally injured by the explosion and died in one of the lifeboats. Another man was also killed by the mine, and a final count found another seven missing. The liner took 30 minutes to sink and all the other passengers and crew members managed to get into the lifeboats and were picked up by escort craft including HMS *Calvi,* which was minesweeping off North Foreland when the mine went off under the liner.

The *Dunbar Castle* was built by Harland and Wolff for Union-Castle in 1930 and her oil engines gave her a top speed of nearly 15 knots. The massive wreck was largely dispersed in 1959 and now stands no more than 3m high in 18m at 51 22 38; 01 36 18E.

353 Cedrington Court. Mined on January 7, 1940 while carrying 7100 tons of much-needed wheat to Britain, this British Standard Ship (the Liberty Ships of World War One) had been built to the "B" type set of plans in 23 weeks and completed as *War Viper* in March 1918, at the Harland and Wolff yard in Belfast. In August 1919 she was renamed the *Cabotia* and then in February 1925, became the *Cedrington Court.* But she was still a British Standard Ship whatever her name – 5160 tons, 412ft long with a beam of 52ft and a draught of 31, single-screw, 2500hp, top speed 11 knots, funnel amidships and bridge ahead of that.

The wheat in her holds was intended to be offloaded at Hull but she never got as far as that, sinking to the soft bottom in 16m at 51 23 02; 01 35 49E. All her crew were saved. She is now very broken and just under 2m proud.

354 Selma. While on her way from Middlesbrough to Nantes with a mixed cargo of 1500 tons of coal, pig-iron and iron plates, this 1654 ton Norwegian steamer hit a mine on October 25,1915 and sank at 51 23 02; 01 34 25E. Now this ship of 270ft long with a beam of 39ft lies upright on a flat seabed at 17m. She is reported by divers to be very broken, and lying in a 2m scour.

355 Rock pinnacle, or part of a wreck. At 51 22 50; 01 30 49E, this one is 3m proud and about 100ft long in 11m.

356 Patch of wreckage. At 51 22 58; 01 30 44E. Some 30ft square and less than 1m high in 11m.

357 HMS Carilon. An Admiralty-requisitioned trawler of 226 tons, she was mined on December 24,1915, at 51 23 26; 01 31 18E. She now lies with her bows to the south-west, very broken but upright and 3m proud of the seabed at 13m.

358 Surrey. A British dredger, being towed by the tug *Exchange* on January 20, 1960, suddenly broke adrift and sank in rough seas at 51 23 30; 01 32 31E. She is now lying north-east, south-west, and 3m proud in 12m.

359 Unknown, at 51 23 38; 01 31 06E. In two parts, but the same ship. One of the sections has a cable leading from it and linking it to the other. Both parts stand 3m proud in 14m.

360 HMS Tourmaline. One of HM's trawlers. This one, completed in 1935, was 641 tons and was off North Foreland when attacked by German aircraft on February 5, 1941. She sank at 51 23 44; 01 31 14E and is today very broken and lying inside her own scour at 15m.

361 Unknown, at 51 24 02; 01 36 19E. A small wreck, only 45ft long, 4m proud in 17m.

362 HMS Fauvette. Was an armed boarding steamer, described as a merchantile fleet auxiliary, during World War One, but before that was quite a famous ship. She was built in 1912 by Sir Raylton Dixon and Co. of Middlesbrough for the General Steam Navigation Co. of 2644 tons, 315ft long with a beam of 44ft and draught of 19. Her 534hp triple expansion engines could give her a top speed of nearly 16 knots.
    When the War broke out she was lying at Bordeaux and brought the entire British colony there home to England. Then she went back and acted as a despatch vessel during the time the French Government remained in Bordeaux. During the Dardanelles campaign she carried troops to and from Gallipoli and Salonika. But on March 9,1916, commanded by Cdr. H.J. Wilson, RNR, she was heading for inspection duty among the shipping in the Thames Estuary when she struck two mines in quick succession off North Foreland. She went down in 4 minutes at 51 24 01; 01 29 00E, taking with her 2 officers and 12 ratings.

Commander Wilson and the rest of the crew got away in two port lifeboats. Today she lies upright and largely intact, with her bow still towards the north, 4m proud and at the edge of an area of sandwaves in 12m.

363 Emile Deschamps. A French auxiliary minesweeper of 349 tons, which sank at 51 24 21; 01 29 21E on June 4, 1940 after hitting a mine while on her way to Britain after escaping from Dunkirk. Today she lies with her bows still towards the west and 2m proud in 12m, though there is a 1m scour almost all around her.

364 Unknown. At 51 24 16; 01 23 23E. A very small wreck almost completely buried and charted as "foul" in 8m.

365 Opal. A barge sunk on October 24,1921, while being sailed from Portland to London. Little remains at 51 24 03; 01 22 03E in 9m.

Dive Services in Kent

Dive Boats

All the following boats have been recommended by Kent area divers. If there are any changes or additions the publisher would like to be informed so that they can be included in later editions of this book.

Dover. *Growler.* Dave Pascall skippers this 32ft hard boat with all electronic gear, licensed for 8 divers.

Bookings: Dave Pascall, 2 Chaucer Crescent, Dover, Kent CT16 2DA. Tel: 0304 822944.

Dover. *Sea-Lift Two.* Diver-skipper Roy Cousens. This 40ft steel workboat has all electronic gear and is licensed for 8 divers.

Bookings: Roy Cousens, Sea-Lift Ltd, The Clock Tower Building, Western Docks, Dover Harbour, Dover, Kent. Tel: 0304 201092.

Dungeness. *Havalook.* Skipper Jerry Oiller is used to locating wrecks for fishing parties, including some which he says are not charted. He operates a 32ft boat, licensed for 8 divers, all electronic gear.

Bookings: Jerry Oiller, 23 Williamson Road, Lydd-on-Sea, Romney Marsh, Kent TN29 9NT. Tel: 0679 66111.

Folkestone by request. *Cirrus.* Though based at Brighton, diver-skipper Tim Bennetto, a very experienced Kent diver, will bring his 33ft turbo Offshore 105 with all electronic gear to Folkestone for a group booking of a week or more. He is licensed for 12 divers.

Bookings: Tim Bennetto, Indigo Charters, 35 Cissbury Avenue, Peacehaven, East Sussex BN10 8TN. Tel: 0273 586445, or mobile on boat: 0860 209367.

Folkestone. One of Kent's best wreck divers, David Batchelor, skippers *Joanne of Sark,* a 37ft dive boat with a 14ft beam. Licensed for 16 divers, all electronic gear, takes a 5.5m RIB out for use as a safety boat.

Bookings: David Batchelor, Burgate, Kingsford Street, Mersham, Ashford Kent. Tel: 0233 639219, or 0227 730928 (work).

Folkestone. *501 Diver,* a 35ft hard-boat owned by Folkestone Branch BSAC. Can be used by special arrangement by a visiting branch.

Bookings: Secretary of Folkestone BSAC, Colin Cole, Water Farm, Stowting,

Ashford, Kent TN25 6BA. Tel: 0303 862401.

Folkestone. Dive boats can be arranged by The Folkestone Sub-Aqua Centre, Arch 5, Tram Road, Folkestone, Kent CT20 1QD. Tel: 0303 255752.

Ramsgate. *Stella Spei.* Skippered by the very experienced local wreck diver Paul Fletcher, this 30ft dive boat, all electronic gear, is licensed for 12 divers.

Bookings: Paul Fletcher, The Ferns, 72 Southwood Road, Ramsgate, Kent CT11 0AL.Tel: 0843 593971.

Rye for Dungeness area wrecks. *Lacer.* Diver John Blight skippers this 34ft stern trawler, all electronic gear, licensed for six divers.

Bookings: Tel: 0797 280263.

Walmer. *Moss Rose.* The boat of very experienced skipper Dave Harris is highly recommended by local divers of Kingsdown BSAC. His boat is a 25ft, all electronic gear, licensed for eight divers.

Bookings: Dave Harris, 32 The Strand, Walmer, Deal, Kent.Tel: 0304 362703.

Walmer. *Morning Haze.* Skipper Dave Chamberlain is one of the most knowledgeable wreck experts in Kent. His boat is a 27ft with all electronic gear, licensed for 8 divers.

Bookings: Dave Chamberlain, 16 North Barrack Road, Walmer, Deal Kent. Tel: 0304 362744.

Air/Equipment supplies

Dover. Dover BSAC. Air by arrangement. Tel: 0304 831264.

Dover. Sea-Lift Ltd., The Clock Tower Building, Western Docks, Dover Harbour, Dover, Kent. Tel: 0304 201092.

Folkestone. The Folkestone Sub-Aqua Centre, Arch 5, Tram Road, Folkestone, Kent CT20 1QD. Tel: 0303 255752.

Folkestone. Folkestone BSAC, Folkestone Yacht and Motor Boat Club, North Street, Folkestone, Kent. Air by arrangement. Tel: 0303 862401.

Gillingham. South East Diving Supplies, 140 Richmond Road, Gillingham, Kent ME7 1LS. Tel: 0634 579624.

Herne Bay. Canterbury BSAC. Air by arrangement. Tel: 0227 455693.

Hythe. Channel Divers, the diving section of the Hythe and Saltwood Sailing Club, The Esplanade, Hythe, Kent. Air by arrangement. Contact: DO, Paul Bratton. Tel: 0233 636194.

Maidstone. Air Services, Beaconsfield Road, Maidstone, Kent. Tel: 0622 758005.

Orpington. Kent Diving, 7 Oasthouse Way, Orpington, Kent BR5 3PT. Tel: 0689 875521.

Ramsgate. Thanet BSAC. The Icehouse, Military Road, Royal Harbour, Ramsgate Kent. Air by arrangement. Tel: 0843 601919.

Sutton-at-Hone. C Sports Ltd, 115 Main Road, Sutton-at-Hone, Dartford, Kent. Tel: 0322 866261.

Weather services

The Met Office now offers several services of use to Kent divers. The general weather for the area is available by telephoning Weathercall on 0898 500 402. This gives the Kent, Surrey and Sussex weather forecast. More important to the diver is Marinecall on 0898 500 456. This gives the weather for Channel East, which covers Selsey Bill to North Foreland and 12 miles offshore.

The latest service from the Met Office is MetFAX Marine, a special dial-up weather operation. The Met Office say about this service: In general you must set your fax machine to POLL RECEIVE mode, without documents in the feeder, before dialling one of our numbers. If your fax machine has a handset, it may be sufficient to pick up the handset, dial one of the numbers, and press the START button after our message. Some fax machines will automatically go into POLL RECEIVE mode if you dial one of the product numbers from your fax machine keypad and press the START button. If you have difficulties, phone the MetFAX information line on 0336 400 500.

You should note, of course, that MetFAX Marine is a premium-rate telephone service, though most material takes 2-5 minutes to transmit.

MetFAX Marine services which will mostly interest the Kent diver are:

The 2-day East Channel Coast forecast and 00/24hr forecast chart, covering North Foreland to Selsey Bill. Fax number: 0336 400 456.

The 3-5-day Channel Waters forecast and 48/72hr forecast chart. Fax number: 0336 400 471.

Note – General weather lore is given in the Dive Planners' Guide at the front of this book.

BSAC branches in Kent

Canterbury. Canterbury BSAC meets at Kingsmead Swimming Pool, Canterbury, on Thursdays at 7pm. This branch of nearly 90 members welcomes visiting divers to dive Kent with them and would like more members. Members are keen wreck divers and the branch owns two RIBs and two "soft" inflatables.
Secretary: Sarah Cook, 35 Copinger Close, Canterbury, Kent CT2 7DJ. Tel: 0227 455693.

Cobham. Thameside BSAC meets at Cobham Hall School, Cobham, on Fridays at 7.30pm. A branch of 20 members and would welcome more. Visiting divers are welcome too. Branch owns fully-equipped dive boat with magnetometer, radio etc.
Secretary: Mr. D.L. Meekings, 115 Lancelot Avenue, Strood, Kent ME2 2YX.

Dartford. North West Kent Branch No.489. Meets at Cobham Hall Girls School, Cobham, on Thursdays at 8pm. Branch has 30 members and would welcome more. Visiting divers welcome. Owns fully-equipped dory with 90hp engine.
Secretary: Mrs. K. Wilson, 240 Crescent Drive, Petts Wood, Kent BR5 1AX. Tel: 0689 821823.

Dover. Dover BSAC meets at Dover Leisure Centre, Dover on Tuesdays at 7.30pm. Has 30 members and would welcome more, particularly experienced divers. Visiting divers welcome with prior notice. Branch owns a fully-equipped Pilot 17 cathedral-hull dory.
Secretary: Mr. M.J. Lawson, 8 The Terrace, Shepherdswell, Dover, Kent CT15 7PX. Tel: 0304 831264.

Downham. Bromley and District BSAC meets at Downham Baths, Downham, on Mondays at 7.30pm. Has 140 members and would welcome more. Visiting divers are welcome. Branch owns three boats – 4m Laros, C5 Bombard and 5m Humber.
Secretary: Mr .M.J. Smith, 54 Portland Road, Bromley, Kent BR1 5BD. Tel: 081-857 0155.

Edenbridge. Edenbridge BSAC meets at Edenbridge Leisure Centre on

Wednesdays at 8pm. Has 73 members and would welcome more. Visiting divers also welcome. Branch owns a Zodiac, but mostly charters hard boats.

Secretary: Dr. J.M. Knights, Westfield Cottages, Cudham Lane, South Cudham, Kent TN14 7QA. Tel: 0959 576364.

Folkestone. Folkestone BSAC meets at Shornecliffe Camp Pool from 6.30pm. to 7pm on Wednesdays. These wet meetings are followed by dry ones at 8.30pm. at the branch's clubhouse at the Folkestone Yacht and Motorboat Club in North Street, Folkestone. Branch has 70 members and is very active using their 2 inflatables and 35ft hard boat. They welcome new members and visiting divers can dive with them.

Secretary: Colin Cole, Water Farm, Stowting, Ashford, Kent TN25 6BA. Tel: 0303 862401.

Gillingham. Medway BSAC meets at Black Lion Sports Centre, Mill Road, Gillingham, at 8.15pm on Mondays. Very active branch with 100 members but would welcome more. Visitors can dive if room on branch's four boats – two Bombard RIBs, one Tornado RIB and one inflatable. Branch has own clubhouse in Prince Arthur Road, Gillingham.

Secretary: Mrs.Janice Booth, 19 Brenchley Road, Gillingham, Kent ME8 6HD.

Gillingham. South East Diving Centre Branch. A BSAC School Branch with 86 members. Has three RIBs. Welcomes visiting divers.

Secretary: Mr. T.C. Knight, 14 Richmond Road, Gillingham, Kent ME7 1LS. Tel: 0634 579624.

Maidstone. Maidstone BSAC meets at Mote Park Pool on Fridays at 9pm. Has 92 members and would welcome more. Branch owns three inflatables and one RIB and has own clubhouse. Visiting divers welcome.

Secretary: David Green, 22 Bournewood Close, Otham, Kent ME15 8TJ. Tel: 0622 861799.

Orpington. Orpington BSAC meets at Walnuts Leisure Centre, Orpington, on Thursdays at 8pm. Orpington has 60 members and would welcome more. Branch owns a Zodiac inflatable.

Secretary: Mrs .K.L. Defraine, 7 Melrose Crescent, Farnborough, Orpington, Kent BR6 9NT.

Ramsgate. Thanet BSAC meets at Ramsgate Swimming Pool, Newington Road, on Wednesdays at 8.30pm. Has 94 members and would welcome more. Visiting divers are welcome. Branch has clubhouse on the first floor of the Icehouse, Military Road, beside the Royal Harbour at Ramsgate. The Icehouse was built in 1870 and was used to store ice brought in bulk from Norway for the Ramsgate fishing fleet! Branch owns one inflatable.

Secretary: Miss A.M .Read, 2A The Cinderpath, Broadstairs, Kent CT11 1NP. Tel: 0843 601919.

Rochester. Kent Nautilus BSAC meets at Sir Joseph Williamson Mathematical School Pool, on alternate Mondays at 7.30pm.

Secretary: Miss V. Bunting, 359 Lower Woodlands Road, Gillingham, Kent.

St. Margaret's Bay. Kingsdown BSAC meets at St. Margaret's Country Club on Tuesdays at 7pm. Has 15 members and owns a Zodiac inflatable.

Secretary: Mr.K.M.Riddell, 14 St.Winifreds Road, Cheriton, Folkestone, Kent CT19 4BW.

Sheerness. Swale BSAC meets at the Sheerness Pool on Saturdays at 5pm. Has 64 members and would welcome more. Visiting divers are welcome too. Branch owns two boats - Humber RIB and Avon Searider.

Secretary: Mr. J. Stanford, 58 Broadway, Sheerness, Kent ME12 1ST.
Sidcup. Bexley BSAC meets at Lamorbey Baths, Sidcup, on Tuesdays at 8pm. Has 65 members and would welcome more. Visiting divers with permission of DO. Branch owns two boats – one RIB and one Humber.

Secretary: Mrs. Mary Nunn, 35 Nightingale Road, Petts Wood, Orpington, Kent. Tel: 0689 838579.

Tunbridge Wells. Tunbridge Wells BSAC meets at St.Johns Swimming Pool, St.Johns Road, on Friday evenings. Has 120 members and would welcome more. Visiting divers can dive with them with prior notice. Branch owns two boats – Humber and Humber Alpha.

Secretary: Dr. S. Domizio, The Flat, 515 Westhorne Avenue, Eltham, London SE9 6DL. Tel: 081-850 1613 (day); 081-859 7299 (evening).

West Wickham. West Wickham BSAC meets at West Wickham Swimming Baths, Station Road, on Thursdays at 7.30pm. Branch has 90 members and would welcome more. Visiting divers welcome to dive with agreement of DO. Branch owns fully-equipped Tornado Offshore Pro with 115hp engine.

Secretary: Emma Dare, 68 Woodpecker Mount, Pixton Way, Croydon, Surrey CRO 9JE. Tel: 081-6514013.

Note– The British Sub-Aqua Club Regional Coach for the South-East, who looks after Kent, is Adrian Clarke, 123 Grand Drive, Herne Bay, Kent CT6 8HS. Tel: 0227 360694. He is available and willing to give advice to divers about any problems they might encounter when diving Kent.

The Military Remains Act

This Act became law on September 8, 1986, and in the future may affect the wreck diver much more than it does at present. The main drive of the Act is to preserve the sanctity of "war graves", that is the wreckage of military ships and aircraft known to contain human remains of servicemen or women.

The wreckage of all military aircraft of any nation is automatically protected by the Act, but naval ships will have to be designated by the Secretary of State and will need a statutory instrument to do so. This means that ships to be named as "war graves" will have to be named and approved by Parliament in the same way that ships to be protected as historic wrecks need a statutory instrument passed through Parliament.

There seems no doubt that those who passed the Act had little idea of the number of ships which could fall under its terms, such as merchant ships with a naval gunner aboard - was he among the survivors? - and as a result no ships have yet been named under the Act. This does not mean that ships are not covered by the general thrust of the Act and divers should therefore treat all possible "war graves" with total respect.

However, once these ships have been named the diver commits an offence only if he or she tampers with, damages, moves, removes, or unearths remains or enters an enclosed interior space in the wreckage. Nothing in the Act prevents the wreck diver from visiting the site, examining the exterior or even settling on the wreckage. An offence is only committed if he or she disturbs remains or enters a proper compartment in the wreck. The punishment on conviction of an offence is a fine. This is, of course, a brief guide to the Act. Serious wreck divers should study the Act itself – your library or HM Stationery Office should be able to supply a copy.

Index

Please note that the following are **site numbers**, not page numbers. Entries in *italic* are names of wrecks.